Reap the Whirlwind

Reap the Whirlwind

Industrial Society Uncontrolled

KARL-HENRIK PETTERSSON

translated by

W. GLYN JONES

SAXON HOUSE

SAXON HOUSE
D. C. Heath Ltd,
Westmead, Farnborough, Hants, England

© 1973 Karl-Henrik Pettersson
First published in Sweden by Bokförlaget Forum AB
as *Det Herrelösa Industri Samhället*
© Translation 1975 D. C. Heath Ltd

ISBN 0 347 00035 5
Printed in Great Britain by the Garden City Press Limited,
Letchworth, Hertfordshire SG6 1JS

Contents

Chapter 1
Introduction

Come mothers and fathers throughout the land
and don't criticise what you can't understand.
Your old road is rapidly aging.
Please get out of the new one if you can't lend a hand.
For the times they are a-changin'.

Bob Dylan

In one of his books, Birger Norman[1] tells of a happy little man living in a wealthy country. He owns a glass egg in which it is always summer, and the weather is always fine, but one day he drops his egg and, when he picks it up, notices a bad smell issuing from the cracks. "Now he could see things which he had never before seen or expected to see."

For many people the industrial society has turned into a similar broken illusion which, viewed more closely, reveals things we never expected to see. Apart from distorted perspectives, unexpected disadvantages and yawning gaps, the very description of it as an affluent society is misleading, dangerous, and imprecise: misleading because unparalleled riches and material affluence exist in shameless proximity to incredible poverty; misleading also since this designation, if we wish to use it, can be applied only to a minority, far less than a third of the world's population. Furthermore, the term is dangerous because it has the power to lull us into the belief that everything is as it should be, and imprecise because material wealth and human and social well-being are by no means identical.

With the aid of technology, man has liberated forces which can carry him to other planets, destroy his own planet at a single blow, or supply at least a minority with a constantly increasing flow of goods and services. However, all this has come about at the expense of a debt to Nature which never has been and perhaps never can be repaid. Our supply of necessities, such as minerals, energy, fresh water and clean air, is coming to an end. The environment is being threatened, damaged and destroyed.

In addition, and irrespective of questions of resources and environment, the highly developed industrial society has characteristics and effects which most people are finding more and more difficult to accept. In both capitalist and socialist economies a pattern has evolved of vast bureaucratic organisations, central planning and the dominion of technology. These characteristics are probably far removed from (even in contrast with) those which the majority of people consider to be important: personal contact and a knowledge of what is going on, decentralisation and self-determination. It is obvious, however, that not everyone is subjected to pressures on all sides, and this can be one of the principal hindrances in seeking to solve the problems.

It is to the ever-increasing speed of technical and economic progress that we should attribute responsibility for what has happened and is happening, a claim based on neither romantic escapism nor a Luddite mentality. There is no denying that the developed industrial society offers mankind the highest material standards ever known, but it also leads rapidly to a narrow cul-de-sac. Space is limited, and despite disagreement as to whether or not we need to apply the brakes, it is absolutely certain that we need to do just that. Whether we consider world population, the use of natural resources, the gross national product of Japan or Volvo's turnover, it is inconceivable that the acceleration in growth can continue: it must be turned into either retardation or stabilisation.

The picture presented by industrial society is so absurd

and distorted that a historical examination of its characteristics and foundations is essential. A backward glance in this
way will cause us to question most of what has been
achieved. Belief in progress and technical development will
be seen as an essentially modern phenomenon. The right of
ownership, so firmly fixed as a tenet of Western society, will
be seen to be open to change. The ambivalent attitude of the
Church towards the growth of capitalism may surprise us
and be recognised as intellectually weak. A historical
analysis of industrialisation will give little support for the
idea that the characteristic pattern of advanced industrial
societies is natural, original or, as many would have it,
sacrosanct. In reality it is rather an unnatural, artificial and
unjust course of events which has firmly set its stamp on
developments only during the past hundred years. Our
departure from the relatively stable, consistent, moderate,
technical and cultural development which was typical of
earlier centuries has been sudden.

When the little man with the glass egg saw the distorted
picture and noticed the evil smell, and when he realised that
what he had thought was summer and sunshine was only an
illusion, he was afraid. "Now he did not want to see any
more!"

Possibly politicians and businessmen react in the same
way as the little man in the story when confronted with the
problems brought about by the developed industrial society:
they do not want to see them. Actions which should be
aimed at the long term are in fact aimed at the short term.
Tactics and an unwillingness to listen are more apparent
than an attempt to work out a comprehensive strategy and
engage in a meaningful discussion. One-sidedness, mutual
contempt and a concentration on appearances are more
characteristic of the debate than comprehensiveness, tolerance and a respect for reality. Perhaps this is not surprising,
since confidence in their own infallibility and a boundless
optimism are the two most obvious traits of both these
groups. When did we last meet a politician who got up and

honestly, without hedging, admitted that he had just made a mistake, or that his own party's attitude to some contemporary problem was poorly formulated or even wrong? How often have we heard an industrialist say that industrial production and technology are leading to the exhaustion of our resources, the destruction of the environment and the alienation of one man from another?

With supreme contempt for anyone else's ideas, the practical politician, denying that the policies thought to be suitable ten years ago are no longer tenable, explains that a growth society is the only good society. The trouble, says Bertil Ohlin in a recent book, is not that we are living in an affluent society with too much consumption. On the contrary, consumption must be increased. As our first priority, he argues, we must seek to increase the *per capita* national income. His conclusion is disturbing – that we should move towards a society with increased production and full employment, which will give most people an ever-increasing and more satisfying standard of consumption.

How much insight into our environment and respect for global resources can be found in this exhortation? If we do act in this way – and in practice this is the attitude, most prevalent among politicians, which determines social developments – how can we arrive at a fair distribution of incomes between developed and under-developed countries? Is it absolutely certain that increased production can in fact be combined with full employment? Rather, is it not true that if technical and economic development continues in the present pattern, we cannot even hope for a society offering employment for everyone in any reasonable sense of the term? No politician so far has stepped forward to say that a yet more advanced industrial society and its technology will inevitably produce increased unemployment, that full employment is no longer our policy or that the industrial development which we unreservedly support will unfortunately lead to the disappearance of jobs. Perhaps, as a politician, he will not, or cannot, see these consequences.

The same reluctance to accept reality is widespread in business. However, the use of short-term tactics, the refusal to accept new proposals, and general unwillingness to discuss matters of principle, can partly be interpreted as expressions of the reaction which has always ensued from a redistribution of power and prestige. During the capitalist epoch, and indeed throughout human history, people have never allowed their power to wane without protest. The feudal barons had to surrender a great deal of their power to the free cities who, some centuries later, had to make way for national states. Craftsmen were forced out by merchant capitalists, who were in their turn edged aside by industrial capitalists, and so on. This whole process has been marked by frustration, protest and considerable violence.

It is little more than 100 years since many industrialists were what we would call "politically radical", for example Richard Cobden, Robert Owen and others who were radical agitators in an established society. Politically, Robert Peel was influenced so greatly by the demands of the industrial society that, in 1846, he voted to repeal the Corn Laws (despite the fact that he was the leader of the British Conservative Party, dominated at the time by wealthy land-owners). Today the picture is quite different. Of course, the conservatism of industrialists is quite consistent and logical. Given a situation in which power and influence are declining, it is probably impossible to give in voluntarily, even if the inevitability of change is realised, and even if it is obvious that respite and respect could be achieved by being willing to take the initiative in making concessions.

Towards the end of the 1960s, the foundations of capitalist economic life were subjected to very severe criticism. The critics, most of them young, maintained that they could not understand why slender resources were not given monetary values in the cost calculations done by business concerns, why important increases in assets were omitted from balance sheets, why a dollar earned on the manufacture of tanks should be as valuable as a dollar earned on toothpaste,

why there is equal freedom to manufacture nerve gas and
vitamin tablets, or why a managing director with independence and job satisfaction should be able to earn a salary of
$150,000 a year.

The questions asked, though provocative and often naïve,
were on the whole well-founded. In this situation two
strategies are possible. One can take up the discussion in
principle and show with factual arguments that such critics
are in the wrong. On the other hand, one can tacitly assume
that the criticism is unjustified, and consequently consider
the questioner to have been led astray by insufficient knowledge and the exaggerations and oversimplifications of the
mass media. Big business chose the second method, and
viewed all criticisms as products of insufficient insight into
the way industry works. In Sweden it was planned to resolve
difficulties by means of more extensive public relations
services, and by expanding the information services of company branch organisations. Conferences dealing with public
opinion were held, in the course of which companies were
taught how best to organise those information activities
aimed at affecting the climate of opinion: formulation of
problems, objectives, priorities and so on. "Answers to
statistics" and "Advice on television interviews" were
distributed to industrial leaders in pocket-book form. In
August 1969 the Association for the Study of Business and
Society arranged a conference in Tylösand. Most of the
leading figures from the Swedish business world attended,
and found among their papers the following thought-
provoking advice about the art of debating: "A good rule is
to be honest on all points, as the listeners can acquire
information from secondary sources."

Possibly, reluctance on the part of businesses to choose
the other and intellectually more attractive strategy simply
reflects the fact that an ideological platform, from which
meaningful discussion can be promoted, no longer exists. It
is symptomatic that the discussions of principle which do
occur from time to time appear, in the main, to be ambiva-

lent and of little interest. The debate becomes stereotypical; it is maintained that freedom from restraints on business, along with free competition, increases efficiency and makes for the maximum use of resources (in comparison with the sub-optimum state of affairs in a socialist economy). Indeed, freedom from restraints on business is seen as a condition of individual freedom (compared with being swallowed up in an anonymous collective). It is often argued, furthermore, that the relation between economic power and political power is made up of a complex system of checks and balances which decreases the likelihood of abuse from either side. The serious question, of course, is whether these traditional liberal theories are still valid.

It is widely known today that global resources are being exhausted, population growth is uncontrolled, famine appears sporadically, unemployment is on the increase, and ordinary people are becoming increasingly disillusioned with the way of life which is consistent with a highly developed industrialised society. Yet this alarming situation is tackled by politicians and leaders of business and industry in a manner which can only be described as evasive, short-sighted and tactical rather than strategic. Scarce resources are used on an even greater scale, and more unnecessary consumer goods appear on the markets. Meanwhile, unemployment figures rise in developed and underdeveloped countries alike, and the gap between rich and poor widens. The steps taken result in only marginal improvements and adaptations irrelevant to the basic problems. The most fundamental question of all – whether we should overcome our difficulties by means of more rapid industrialisation – is scarcely heeded, certainly not by politicians and businessmen.

This reminds us again of the man with the glass egg, who was scared and did not want to look. He pasted over the cracks and said, "Now we must remember to be careful. . . . This must not happen again."

One has an intuitive feeling that the complete truth is yet to be revealed. Politicians and businessmen are undoubtedly intelligent, industrious and respectable men and women who are aware of the fundamental problems. Yet despite this awareness they do nothing to avert the danger; instead, they talk of the harsh economic reality whose conditions we all have to accept, irrespective of social philosophy. They speak of ever-increasing international interactions, and of the conflict experienced by all politicians between what they would like to do for their own countries and the possibility of doing it in a world where competition plays an ever greater role. Any individual country's political and economic freedom of action is so limited, they maintain, that it is usually forced to follow international developments. If this is the case, then the somewhat disturbing conclusion is that other countries must be in the same situation, which in a global perspective means that all states, to a greater or lesser extent, are bound by uncontrolled development. This is an absurd thought.

There is a general fear that industrialised society is uncontrolled, that technical and economic development is now ruling man and his institutions – nations, businesses, organisations. Thus this book is primarily concerned with the dynamic aspects of the advanced industrial society, and it is an attempt to decide whether technological innovation is governed by criteria and conditions which, in any acceptable sense, can be said to reflect human needs, and to be reasonable given the availability and distribution of resources. It will be shown that the industrialised society subordinates need to the demands of its own apparatus, that technology consumes increasingly large amounts of already scarce resources at a constantly high rate, and continues to be a burden on the environment, and that the distribution of incomes, in the long run, actually shows signs of becoming less equitable. Consequently, the book is also an attempt to define those measures necessary, in the short time available, to control developments which it has not yet been possible to control, let alone to restrain.

The first task is to analyse and discuss the advanced industrial society with a so-called mixed economy; this will

be referred to as a capitalist society, not from any particular
ill-will, but simply because the essential characteristic of a
capitalist economy – the decentralised right to dispose of a
certain proportion of profits made – is still present and
represents the fundamental difference from a socialist
economy, in which profits are distributed by a central
organisation. It is scarcely necessary to point out that this
distinction, theoretically, makes "capitalism" possible in a
society in which the means of production are in public
ownership, and "socialism" possible in a society where the
means of production are in private hands.

Such subjective elements as there are in the book result
from its being an expression of the author's own knowledge,
experience and basic point of view rather than an attempt
to assess other, conflicting approaches.

The fundamental values on which the discussion rests
should be made clear. Briefly, the analysis is based on three
central tenets: reality is preferable to an image of reality, the
whole is more important than the parts, and quality is more
important than quantity.

Reality and images of reality

It perhaps seems a truism today to argue that reality is
preferable to an image of reality or, what is really the same
thing, that a map is a poor substitute for a landscape.
However, the distinction is not always clear to everyone, and
in talking of the industrialised society it is essential to
identify the images we use in making judgements and
decisions. It might be that they are not only consciously and
unnecessarily imperfect, but also that they conflict with
reality. If abstractions are not to become laws unto themselves, a constant watch must be kept on them. This is not
always understood, yet the sovereignty of reality depends on
the image always being regarded with the same suspicion
evinced about a story in which the listener does not believe.

We are speaking of images of complex social realities, intended to describe and to influence. At the simplest level, such processes are a function of language, the spoken word. It has been said that words are approximations, and although this may be a commonplace notion, it is still important – especially when we realise that concepts and ideas have often come to be seen as more significant than the realities from which they issue. Words are always suspicious. We have to ask what is hidden behind concepts such as "maximum profit", "profitability", "the social responsibility of industry", "investment calculations", and "industrial democracy". Suppose someone makes the statement, for example, that efficiency is the key to the world's problems. We need to know just what is meant by the word "efficiency". For a businessman making such a statement, "efficiency" probably means the rational use of labour and capital in a given situation and, furthermore, is likely to be closely associated with such notions as the ability to organise, work discipline, and technical development. However, efficiency can also mean selectivity, economy, reclamation, three types of washing powder instead of thirty-three.

The image always bears the mark of the man who creates it. All abstractions of reality are subjective in the sense that values, knowledge and experience inevitably affect the result. Whose values and ideas create the "objective" picture of a firm included in its annual report? Ludwig von Mises, one of the best known of modern liberal ideologists, argues that "liberalism is based on pure scientific principles, on economic knowledge and sociology which, within their systems, do not allow evaluation: their task is to determine what the position is and how it developed." Von Mises should have listened to his ideological forefather John Stuart Mill, who said that "objective" truths exist only in very small numbers, and perhaps not at all. According to Mill, the decision as to what is true is based on one's own universe, and pure chance decides on which of these universes he

• •

relies. What represents progress to a director might well be the opposite to his employees.

It is vitally important, therefore, to look behind images and see what they really represent. At the same time, however, while it is wrong not to make a clear distinction between a symbol and what it symbolises, it is equally wrong to ignore the interplay between the image and reality. This would hide the dynamism in the simple model: $reality_1$ – $image_1$– $reality_2$– $image_2$. This is perhaps the most important of Marxist arguments. In the model, the image takes over and tends to reduce the wealth and extent of natural variety which exists in reality.

A recent book on future prospects, limited by the fact that it expresses the point of view of an industrial organisation, explains why the shape of changes to come will be so convenient:

> "The studies of future patterns . . . can contribute to answering the question of how far human beings are capable of consciously exploiting future possibilities and avoiding future crises, and to what extent they will continue to be at the mercy of their inability to bring about change."

Such a remark is symptomatic, since the definition of the task is diffuse and misleading. It should be clearly stated that although the studies of future prospects in this context are only part of the firm's attempts to make maximum profit, such studies can also be undertaken in an attempt to control a more and more uncontrollable reality.

In the longer term we move from almost complete certainty towards increasing uncertainty, and in this situation a well-thought-out strategy will come to mean strength, in so far as it transforms uncertainty into certainty or at least into calculable risk. However, prognoses which reflect future reality can, through multiplicity and interaction, eventually reduce society's flexibility. Prognoses can become self-fulfilling prophecies in which predictions are based on what is profitable today, or what the Rand Corporation and the Hudson Institute think is going to happen. Judgement should be reserved in the face of such studies.

The whole is more important than the parts

This means that the consequences of any measures or activities undertaken should be studied beyond their own limits, and that the justification and value of an action should be judged according to its total effect. The extent to which different part systems are dependent on each other should be made clear, and estimates, assumptions or descriptions, in which interplay with society as a whole is either not apparent or is concealed, should be questioned. "The whole" should be defined from one case to another, encompassing all the part systems which can reasonably be said to be affected by a certain phenomenon. In other words, if we are to describe, measure and control any activity, this must be from a base where at least the principal consequences of an action are apparent. The spreading ripples issuing from new possibilities, and the effects which some changes will bring about must be followed as far as possible so that they can be evaluated and contained, irrespective of the consequences predicted by the system when the change took place. In its most trivial, concrete form, this will impel us to realise that the implications of advanced industrialisation can only be judged and properly controlled in a global perspective and with an eye to global influences.

The national state persists, despite the fact that it is becoming outmoded, because people still tend to identify themselves in relation to their closest geographical neighbours (on whom their existence partly depends), and political control continues to presuppose geographical proximity. Any discussion of the developmental tendencies of the industrial society is pointless if the conclusions are limited to a long-term plan for industrial policy in one country alone. It is not unreasonable to ask what is to happen to the advanced industrialised society as a social phenomenon in the course of future decades, since it appears inevitable that national political peculiarities and ambitions, as well as ideological conflicts between different economic systems, will be erased and replaced by cohesive international structures. The forces moving in this direction are quite invincible.

Perhaps the most characteristic and unfortunate peculiarity of the developed industrialised society is our incapacity to see reality as it is. A contributary cause may be the use of images which are either inappropriate to the age or insufficiently comprehensive and complete. However, the most important reason lies in the models, predictions and aims which are only pertinent within a limited sphere, the total picture and the reactions of all the surrounding areas to be affected being simplified or ignored. "Uncertainty absorption" is the theorist's term for the trivial observation that the director never hears the whole truth from his subordinates because the information has been sifted on its way up through the organisation, but there are far more subtle and significant reasons for a failure to transmit information. For example, reality might well be emasculated if expressed in substantive terms:

"There is a bad atmosphere in the firm."
"Who says?"
"Svensson, the foreman."
"Oh him, he is always making trouble."

Here the real situation has been fragmented and obscured because it has been related to a particular individual.

The whole of our social pattern is based on a distribution of work and profit which makes specialisation and fragmentation much more natural than versatility and integration. Insight into everything going on is a rare phenomenon, and influence extending over the whole of an organisation virtually unknown. Staffan Seeberg makes the main character in one of his novels[2] (a scientist, carrying out research into

nerve gas for a multinational company, who in the course of
time has begun to have doubts about his work) reflect on the
responsibility of the research worker:

> "I might say that I am serving knowledge and then
> carry on playing around in my secluded little corner
> without paying attention to broader considerations, or
> to the total perspective in which our gases are sprayed
> over jungles, plains and fields to kill animals and men. I
> could quietly get on with my research, our scientific
> knowledge. Why should I look for any connection
> between objective scientific knowledge and these un-
> pleasant perspectives? . . . Let scientific knowledge, in
> all its multitudinous forms, continue as before, just in
> the same way as our individual lives, disorganised and
> unplanned like fragments and coloured tiles, odd bits of
> planks floating around without any connection with
> their surroundings."

This is pursuing the idea to its logical conclusion. The
research worker is surrounded by a community of men and
women, and his achievements are evaluated in this narrow
circle, according to its norms. Rewards are linked to the
standards valid within a part system, not to the wider consequences which the work will have outside. The technical
beauty, originality and general validity of the results are of
far greater significance in deciding the way forward than are
needs, the possibility of utilising the results, and their
ultimate effects.

The industrialised society is in fact so divided within itself
that we are inclined to regard this as the natural state of
affairs. A social anthropologist writes that she was taken
aback when a South American Indian woman asked her how
glass beads are made in our civilisation. Uncertain how to
reply, she eventually said, "We make them from sand." The
Indian woman thought for a moment and then said, "Come,
let us make some glass beads." This trivial occurrence
demonstrates the strength and weakness of a society based

on far-reaching specialisation. Access to all kinds of things does not necessitate a knowledge of their background, but at the same time we lose the assurance derived from a more generalised knowledge.

The typical pattern in the fragmented industrialised society is rather like this: I look after my own affairs. You look after yours. Pressure and counter-pressure. Control and counter-control. Balance. The task of the research worker is to produce or to adapt knowledge, while it is taken for granted that politicians (or others) will decide the extent to which the products are ethical or necessary. Firms must develop, produce and sell (which corresponds anyway to their abilities and wishes) within the framework provided by society. It has been called a "pass-the-buck" society, but it cannot continue in this way.

The distinction between tasks and responsibilities results in a very complicated situation when an attempt is made to define reality. What makes the picture even more complex is the relationship between different part systems which is so characteristic of the advanced industrialised society. We are faced with a confused network of links keeping the entire economic system together and making it function. We get lost if we analyse a portion of the whole and then draw general conclusions. Awareness of this fundamental error can often lead to a useful analytical insight when attempting to describe the industrialised society in greater detail.

Quality before quantity

This only means asking ourselves *what* – rather than *how much* – is made. The contents of a firm's product-range rank higher than the size of the organisation, and the criteria determining, for instance, the choice of products and the kinds of investments made become an important focus of study. It has been said that technical development is blind; it does not distinguish between right and wrong, or between good and evil. With technological development now more rapid than ever, this realisation must lead us to examine the mechanisms and forces governing its course. To place technological development under democratic control, in the true sense of the word, is not only desirable but necessary, but it is difficult to carry out within the framework of present-day industry. It is paradoxical that examples of institutionalised and well-established contact between producer and customer are difficult to find in the fields of military and space technology. To bring technological possibilities efficiently into line with needs seems to be difficult, but it is high time it was done.

Chapter 2
The age of the economic life-span

I am in touch with an American sailor and ask why his country builds ships which last for such a short time. He replies, seriously, that such great progress is made each day in the art of navigation that even the most magnificent ship would be obsolete if it lasted more than a certain number of years. These words – on a specialised subject, but coming naturally from a man of humble birth – indicate the fundamental idea on which a great nation bases all its objectives.

Alexis de Tocqueville

Can it really be that in a greater, global perspective, mankind is not in control of technological development? There seem to be many indications that this is so.

The image of the train to Hell, in which all the passengers have been condemned to complete helplessness, has often been used. To jump off would be impossible, or at least it would be madness and doomed to failure. Furthermore, under no circumstances would it solve the problems for those left behind, who are almost certainly in the majority. To sit and do nothing is, of course, possible, but in this case we either know that the catastrophe is inevitable, or else remain blissfully ignorant of what is coming. Both situations are absurd, yet even if we are prepared to try it does not seem possible to make contact with whoever is allowing the train to accelerate to a breakneck speed. Since we cannot identify this person we find ourselves in a fiendish dilemma.

One of the most remarkable things about people's attitudes towards the forces in control of developments is their unwillingness or inability to formulate their thoughts clearly. More often than not, this problem is not touched on at all, or if it is, the manner of discussion is invariably limited, vague, naïve or even false. The analysis of any subject clearly reflects the author's own knowledge, experience and position. Sociologist Raymond Aron, plasma physicist Hannes Alfvén, social philosopher Herbert Marcuse, politician Alva Myrdal, and Rolf Edberg, author and civil servant, can be classed as good spokesmen for those who have considered the question of the innate strength of technology and the repercussions of present-day developments. These writers put forward different explanations for what is going on, and they all regard the current trend with misgivings and fear. It is therefore amazing that with so much experience, intelligence and analytical ability, they cannot reach any kind of agreement in this analysis of causes, let alone convince others that their explanations are correct. The picture they produce is a confused one in which it is just possible to discern two principal lines of thought regarding the problem of uncontrolled technological development.

The first is slightly romantic, and avoids the direct issue. Raymond Aron believes that the fault can be located in man himself. The individual's fundamental attitudes determine the dynamic character of technological progress; these attitudes in turn are conditioned by three qualities, namely, his general interest in science and technology, his habit of classifying, calculating and analysing, and his desire for progress and change. It is as though there were some independent force in technology moving towards a never-ending crescendo, says Rolf Edberg, who also hints at a more profound explanation in suggesting that the urge for growth, and its appetite for material things, goes back to a mechanism developed at the time when men's lives were

difficult and dangerous. When the primate descended from
the tree, the struggle for existence demanded evey conceivable effort. Since then this genetically determined avidity
has moved into the affluent society with its countless artificial needs.

Alva Myrdal argues that there is something wrong with
progress when it is possible to observe, in many fields, that
man's power over Nature is increasing at a rapid and even
breathtaking speed, while his power over his own society,
attitudes and institutions does not appear able to keep pace.
There seems to be no authority capable of weighing one
form of progress against other possible forms. Rolf Edberg
is even more pessimistic, and states that if we are to give
ourselves a chance, we must immediately rethink certain
elementary relationships between ourselves and the world
about us. We must prevent catastrophe by ceasing to do
things merely because it is possible for us to do them; we
must slow down the insatiable rush for further growth.

The analysis, then, is lucid and the pessimism well-
founded. However, there is no convincing explanation as to
why progress is getting out of hand, and consequently it
remains impossible to formulate a concrete programme of
action. A certain desire for change and material things, a
certain curiosity and an urge to systematise are probably
human characteristics, but there are good grounds for
questioning their validity as an explanation of the existence
of an economic system which does not distinguish between
aspirins and powerful therapeutic drugs. Can mankind's
interest in science and technology really explain why the
wealthy, industrialised countries developed synthetic fibres
and synthetic coffee despite the catastrophic repercussions
these developments were bound to have on the economies of
the underdeveloped countries producing the raw products?
Hardly – the connection can scarcely be so simplistic.

Contrasting with this first category of attitudes there is
another more optimistic and naïve outlook expressed in such
questions as: Why do we not disarm when everyone hates

war? Why does the population explosion continue when
medical science knows how to stop it? Why must one half of
the world go hungry when the other half has more than
abundant stocks, and when the means of transporting them
are available? The implication is that the chance of achieving
something is there, that the technical resources are known
and available, but that for some reason nothing is done. In
his novel, *The Great Computer*,[3] Olof Johannesson (the
pseudonym used by Hannes Alfvén) can only see one
reasonable explanation for all this – the incompetence of
politicians.

Herbert Marcuse extends this accusation to encompass
the entire political structure of the Western world and the
manner in which Western society functions, rather than
laying the blame at the feet of the people who are working
within its framework. He believes that the connection
between increasing production and increasing destruction,
the game of chance with annihilation, the persistence of
abject poverty amidst unprecedented wealth, all form the
basis for the most objective criticism. Contemporary society
appears to have a built-in mechanism for the inhibition of
social change – that is to say, qualitative change which
would lead to different institutions, a re-arrangement of the
production processes, and a new and more dignified manner
of life. As Marcuse would put it, this means of preventing
social change is perhaps the most characteristic feature of
the advanced industrial society.

Alfvén and Marcuse argue from an emotional standpoint,
but with deep insight and great consistency. Emotional
commitment is often characteristic also of those who try to
argue that the entire question is false and merely represents
a re-statement of the usual old liberal criticism; they believe
that an open market and free competition ensure that
development is determined by the consumer and his needs,
and that technology is essentially produced and fashioned by
consumer demand.

A more subtle argument maintains that the free market is

certainly not perfect, but this can be ignored since the needs
of society are still expressed via the social environment.
Important progress in research presupposes new thinking
and a re-structuring of what experience tells us, and it
seems very likely that new thinking is dependent on the
intellectual and social environment as a whole.

However, "social environment" is a rather misleading
concept, since the needs it has expressed in practice often
reflect military, colonial, and monopolistic interests as opposed to human needs in any qualitative sense. Historically,
technological development appears to be led primarily by
technological, economic and political power groups rather
than by social environment. Positive need might possibly be
a factor, but it is not the most important.

That everything is perfectly satisfactory, that pessimism
and despondency are out of place, or that progress follows a
path laid down by society as a whole, cannot be acceptable
or convincing viewpoints. A thirst for knowledge, an urge
for change and a belief in progress might well be fundamental preconditions, but an explanation of the accelerating
technological developments and the direction which they are
taking is probably to be found much nearer home. It might
well be that the chain of cause and effect (naturally un-
broken) originates from an unproven assumption that the
forces leading these developments are first and foremost
economic. A clue as to the criteria upon which industry's
decisions to replace old capital by new are based, might be
found by means of a close study of how a firm's decisions
on investment are dictated in practice.

The replacement of old capital

The object of investment calculations is to give the decision-
makers in any firm a quantitative measurement for the
financial implications of alternative investments. The anti-
cipated annual surplus and the difference between income

and expenditure for the new project, are measured in relation to the size of the investment. More often than not it is a simple operation of dividing the total investment by the expected profit, when the result (i.e. the period needed to break even) will be a pointer to its financial attractiveness. Theoretically, at least, the end product of the calculations is the basis on which decisions are made.

However, empirical studies of the way in which decisions affecting industrial investment are actually made give a completely different picture. There is such a gap between what might be expected in theory and what emerges in practice that it cannot be bridged by traditional explanations and excuses, however well formulated these may be. It is no use moralising – if only because the observer has an intuitive feeling that the decisions on investments were, after all, not completely ridiculous when seen in context. However, we cannot fail to be surprised when we observe that systematic evaluations of investments are not always undertaken, even when the sums at stake are very large indeed. It can be shown that the vast majority of firms tend to choose the simplest methods of calculation from the large variety of more or less sophisticated techniques available to them. Furthermore, in many cases the decision is still taken even if the calculations do not indicate the investment to be worthwhile. Sometimes the factual basis of the calculations is questioned; it may be suggested that qualitative advantages could emerge which have not yet been revealed, or it will perhaps be argued that profitability can only be achieved through manipulating the parameters of the model. The parameter most easily altered is length of life.

Swedish empirical studies, carried out independently at different times, and largely complementary to each other, mainly support this view. Furthermore, research in the United States, Great Britain, West Germany and France suggests that the position is an international one.

Thus it might well appear that companies in highly developed capitalist societies decide to replace old equip-

ment with new without having first established a firm basis
for doing so. The conclusion must be that even higher
profitability for individual firms, and a far more rapid
expansion of the economy as a whole, could be achieved if
companies could be persuaded to work more systematically
with more reliable calculations. The stage might then con-
ceivably be reached where the technologists' natural
enthusiasm for the potential of a new breakthrough would
not be allowed to influence the ultimate decision in any way
and, indeed, where rational financial criteria were seen as
the only decisive factors. Although such a conclusion now
appears to be correct, the passage of time will almost certainly
show it to be wrong.

The true answer must be that, when seen collectively, the
obvious lack of interest in investment calculations, the tendency to ignore their results when necessary in order to
bring about investment, and the preference for trivial as
opposed to sophisticated investment research techniques are
not a manner of behaviour which can be generally criticised
or rejected but, on the contrary, represent the only sensible
way to proceed, given the company's current situation. The
right way in present circumstances is not represented by
cautious financial calculations, but by the generally optimistic
judgement of the technologists. It is also perfectly reasonable to argue that the models used for the calculations are
likely to be imperfect even at their best. The criticism which
can be levelled at companies merely reflects our general
tendency to believe that the image of reality, the profitability
indicated by the calculations, is reality itself.

The correct diagnosis has yet to be made. Why do firms
so often behave, *vis-à-vis* investment calculations, in the
ways discussed above? If we list the explanations offered by
specialist literature in this field, the answer might begin to
emerge.

First, there are various types of investment which cannot
be decided purely on the basis of the companies' finances.
For example, there is obviously no point in considering the

profitability of an investment which must be carried out for
social, security, or other reasons. Second, it can be shown
that the poorer the prospects of profits, the more calculations are likely to be made. On the other hand, a company
with high liquidity, which has bright prospects and exper-
iences no difficulty in financing projects, will probably see
little point in carrying out a calculation of profitability.
Third, the basis on which such calculations could be made
might be regarded as unreliable. So little is known about
future prices, wages, use of capacity, etc. that it appears
pointless to spend time and resources on calculations.
Management training also plays some part, and the continuous increase in the number and size of investments in
non-material   projects – training,   market   organisation,
systematisation of the administration, and particularly
technological research and development of products –
provides a further explanation. No methods of calculation
are capable of giving a fair assessment of the profitability of
investments of this kind.

However well-founded, these reasons do not provide the
whole answer. There are many investments which are
motivated by neither security nor social requirements, are
not investments in research and development, and are not
carried out in a period of low liquidity or recession by a
company with the administrative resources and information
necessary to undertake well-founded calculations. Despite
all this, investment calculations are often given only marginal significance in the decision-making process.

The real explanation becomes apparent when lack of a
precise profitability calculation is accompanied by a cry of
"invest or perish". For firms engaged in business closely
related to fashion, this has long been a tangible and harsh
reality; failure to acquire a new machine necessary to keep
up with modern fashion trends can well mark the beginning
of financial ruin. The firm limps on behind the others, loses
its share of the market, and in the future may well find it
difficult or even impossible to catch up with competitors.

Similarly, where investment may often be used to introduce some new technology which makes production possible at greatly reduced prices or leads to new products of such improved quality that older lines are superseded, any company which decides not to keep up with competitors' development investments is likely to find itself ruined. A striking example of this kind is the unique position achieved by Pilkington Brothers through their production of high quality glass. A new method of production, introduced in 1958, is considered to be so superior to other processes of plate-glass manufacture that every competitor of any importance has been forced to make licensing agreements with Pilkingtons and thereby to make heavy investments. This is the "invest or perish" situation taken as far as it can go.

Sometimes, argues Professor Erik Lundberg, it must appear to be a kind of snobbery when a manufacturer talks of working out the profitability assessment for a vast new scheme on the back of an envelope over a cup of coffee after lunch, but this is not always so, despite the fact that he may be referring to risky investments in innovative projects. "Even though the desire to shock or tease an economist, believing in a well-organised world of companies basing themselves on rational calculations, is considerable, I believe that profitability calculations in these cases are often of little significance in comparison to a belief in flair."

When it comes to companies' investments in a new technology, it appears to be more a question of when than of whether. Consequently, emphasis is not laid on the assessment of profitability, but on thorough calculations concerning financing and liquidity. The procedure in one multi-national Swedish firm also indicates that the question of resources is given prominence. Detailed long-term predictions taking into account present capacity and increased capacity requirements are employed. The routine presupposes a well specified list of investment requirements for every decision-making unit in the concern – subsidiary companies, sectors, etc.– but only rarely is an assessment of the profitability of the new project proposed. If there is one, it is usually only an internal pay-off assessment. On the other hand, detailed and carefully calculated plans for financing, and predictions on liquidity have to be worked out for the period under consideration. The only reasonable explanation is that, within the framework of the resources available, it is, practically speaking, always profitable to invest.

In many cases it no longer appears to be the technical life-span – the period during which the object of investment can fulfil the technical demands made on it, given normal repair and maintenance costs – which determines when the company should begin to seek or decide to buy new equipment. The physical wear on old machines is no longer the only factor taken into account when deciding whether or not it will be profitable to invest in a new plant. In other words, the period over which it is financially advantageous to use the plant – i.e. its economic life-span – for the reason it was bought, seems increasingly to be shorter than the technical life-span. In any investment situation where the old existing plant is compared with the new, a company must not only take into account the expense of any physical wear necessitating maintenance and repairs, but also the economic cost created by the superior efficiency of the new technology in comparison with the old. Money is lost when the maximum use is not made of the best equipment obtainable.

Economic wear and economic life-span are of course everyday notions to most people living in a highly developed industrial society. In one sense, through a sort of psychological-economic process, all the new things which we are constantly being offered rapidly make what we already possess appear out-of-date and ripe for replacement. Returns from the old object sink below the acceptable level when we consider resources and alternatives, and the same situation applies to industrial investment. Economic wear thus becomes a function of the company's failure to make use of the most modern equipment on the market.

The mathematician and philosopher Norbert Wiener

refers in one of his books to Oliver Wendell Holmes' poem on the one-horse carriage. This distinguished means of transport was apparently so well constructed that, after it had been in use for a century, no single part – wheels, roof, axles, seats – was more heavily worn than any other. The one-horse carriage, says Wiener, really represents the supreme achievement of engineering, and this is no light-hearted fantasy. If the rims of the wheels had lasted a little longer than the axles, their economic value might have depreciated without the durability of the carriage as a whole having been reduced, or else the value of the remaining parts which wore out more quickly might have been reduced. "In point of fact, no product without the qualities of the one-horse carriage is economically constructed." Although tempting, Wiener's conclusion is not entirely correct. He is talking about the optimal life-span, which only involves physical wear. However, the idea of using a one-horse carriage today as a means of transport, even if it still fulfils its technical function, is an anachronism which highlights the factor of economic wear, something which Wiener ignores.

A conceptual distinction between technical and economic life-span is a useful aid in analysing the strength of what is probably the most familiar argument in this discussion – that concerning the built-in obsolescence of capital equipment. A number of weak links – such as soft material, an insecure fastening, bad joints, inability to stand up to knocks – which eventually break, constitute the basic principle. A less brutal technique leads to a general deterioration in appearance when the paint peels, fittings drop off and so on, thus giving the owner a feeling of dissatisfaction.

It is, of course, feasible that close examination of a product would show that some vital component has been skimped, and that a different construction would have prolonged the life-span. However, it is not at this point that the built-in obsolescence accusation is open to criticism. The second stage of reasoning – that skimping and weak

construction or the unsuitable choice of materials are immoral acts – calls for debate.

In fact, this second stage is a mistake, arising principally
from an inability to distinguish between technical and economic life-spans. The consumer has a preference for new
things which he acts upon without stopping to consider
whether or not the old articles he has are worn out. This
factor could only be ignored in an entirely theoretical
society. Likewise, in a fragment of a real society it is possible
to criticise a firm which consciously lowers the technical
quality and thereby the life-span of one of its products.
However, so long as we have a system in which psychological and other non-rational factors combine with new and
increasingly effective technological achievements to force
both consumer and manufacturer constantly to buy new
goods (irrespective of whether or not the old ones are still
usable), then any moral criticism of this nature should be
expressed cautiously and circumspectly. From the point of
view of managers and manufacturers there is no valid
reason to produce goods that will last longer than the
economic life-span, even if this period is shorter than the
technical life-span. This might appear exceedingly immoral
to a cynical observer, but it is only good economic sense for
the company, and is also reasonable from the standpoint of
social economy. A completely different question, of course,
is whether a social system that encourages us to make bad
use of available materials, and to scrap or throw away things
which function perfectly well, can be defended or, indeed,
whether it can be allowed to persist.

That technical development throughout the ages is a
continuous process, possibly even linear, is an interesting
assumption when considering the technical standard of the
capital resources in society. In this perspective, and particularly if limited to industrial capital, it is probably valid to
assert that innovations come relatively indiscriminately and
that technical progress, measured in efficiency per unit of

capital, is continuous. However, if the lack of technical development in this sense is constantly rising, it can also be demonstrated that the economic life-span is reduced with each new achievement; in practice the economic depreciation period for the chain of investments in social economy becomes increasingly shorter.

This is a surprising and challenging discovery, because – assuming the subject we are studying takes in a sufficiently long period, and the technical quality (and thus the life-span) of the capital employed is not consciously reduced – it suggests that, theoretically, it should be possible to indicate a time when the technical life-span of industrial capital as a whole no longer determines what is economical when it comes to disposing of old equipment. Once this point has been passed, the economic life-span which, hitherto, had generally been identical to the technical life-span, would become increasingly shorter. Articles which were in perfect working order would, to an ever greater extent, be under-used or even completely discarded.

An assertion as imprecise as this provides plenty of scope for misinterpretation and criticism. However, the intuition that this hypothesis is correct makes it natural to pursue this train of thought; hence it is possible to formulate two theses for discussion:

(1) the need to consider the economic wear in every calculable investment situation is, historically speaking, a relatively new experience for manufacturers;

(2) the importance of economic wear is tending to increase still further.

If it is possible to prove these suggestions, or even to show that they are probably correct, then there is every reason for careful reflection. Such proof could indicate that the industrial society is caught up in a vicious circle of increased growth, accelerating use of resources, intensified destruction of the environment etc., and that it has no chance of stopping or even of reducing the pace.

The question is whether or not we have already reached this point.

Quantitative madness

Seen in a historical perspective, rapid technological and economic advances are relatively new phenomena. As has often been pointed out, belief in progress is in sharp contrast to most of our religious traditions, which argue that the ideal world is not to be found in this life. The Church does not reward virtue with anything marketable among the princes of this world, rather with bills to be honoured in heaven. Catholic, Protestant and Jew all agree that this earth is not a place where we can expect to find unfailing happiness.

Modern scholars tend to think of the Middle Ages as an intermediate period in social and technological progress, whereas historians seem to agree that the changes and adaptations which were taking place in many fields were a preparation for subsequent developments. For instance, the Gospels and the Church Fathers condemned worldly wealth, and at first the Church regarded money-lending for interest as the worst form of worldly greed. This approach persisted in a lightly modified form throughout the first half of the Middle Ages, but was gradually transformed into an attitude which in many ways was the direct opposite.

The rationalism which characterised Enlightenment philosophy in the eighteenth century had a great influence on technological progress. It was felt that all actions should be dictated by reason, and not principally by religious concepts as had hitherto been the case. This inherently revolutionary point of view was in the sharpest conceivable contrast to the medieval concept based on the principle of maintaining the *status quo*. In practice, the guild system applied a veto against technological progress, partly because of the extremely complicated rules governing production, and partly on account of the basic philosophy that no artisan should

aim to excel over others; indeed it was contrary to accepted
practice that an artisan should try to introduce new
methods. The intense urge to improve society, which now
came in its place, found expression in what Eli F. Heckscher
calls a golden age of cranks.

During the last years of the eighteenth century, therefore,
it is possible to discern the first signs of technological
development and belief in progress, though these changes
had no effect whatever on the life-span of the existing
technology; the twentieth century was well started before
that came out. It is thought-provoking that it took Caesar
about as long to travel from Rome to Paris as it did
Napoleon! Although wooden warships were not technically
identical to earlier vessels in every respect, the patterns
followed well into the nineteenth century were not vastly
different from those used in the seventeenth, and could
boast "ancestors" stretching centuries back into history.
"One of Columbus' sailors could have been a tolerably able
man on Farragut's ship and even a member of the crew of
the ship carrying St Paul to Malta, and he could have felt
quite at home on the quarterdeck of one of Joseph Conrad's
vessels." Apart from one minor improvement, the rifle used
in the American Civil War was identical to that used at
Waterloo fifty years previously.

However, more rapid developments have occurred during
recent decades. At the turn of the century Swedish military
forces had their training based on the Mauser M 96 rifle, the
same weapon used for basic rifle practice in the 1960s. It is
inconceivable, however, that a soldier in 2020 should be
using the same weapon.

The so-called Industrial Revolution can be traced back to
the intellectual advances of the eighteenth century, but it is
not so much the result of scientific and technological
advances influencing industrial production and the crafts,
as the product of a changed intellectual atmosphere culmin-
ating in a new willingness to progress. Newton's scientific
discoveries and the new methods he introduced into

mechanics, optics and mathematics had been accepted by the beginning of the eighteenth century, although scarcely used outside the field of astronomy. He and his contemporary scientists had little if any influence on industrial aims or methods of production, with one well-known exception: James Watt's steam engine was not a stroke of fortune, but the result of years of systematic scientific experiments with an already existing but ineffective technology which was improved and applied by means of the best manufacturing processes known to that age. Watt was the exception who heralded developments destined to be achieved within less than a hundred years.

The most important technical innovations between 1870 and the First World War, such as low current techniques, motor cars, chemical-technical products and so on, no longer arose as the concrete results of brilliant ideas, but resulted from determined research into scientific and technological problems. The major industrial concerns in Germany (Siemens, Krupp, Daimler, Bayer, etc.) appointed "dozens and at times even hundreds of engineers to carry out experiments with new methods and to develop new products".

Methodical industrial research aimed at a specific goal and based on scientific principles is then a generally accepted phenomenon belonging exclusively to the twentieth century. The intensity and breadth of industrial research and development today leads to the conclusion that the relative extent of earlier efforts to bring about progress was far less, and that the essential difference between progress in the present and the late nineteenth century is one of type rather than of degree.

Only fifty years ago, an observer would have found it incredible, if not positively suspect, that industrial concerns should, almost without exception, seek to renew and improve the range of their products and their production methods by means of their own research and development work, or by licensing or patent agreements. The idea that plant replacement for technological reasons was necessary for the profitability and even the existence of a company, was scarcely accepted until after the end of the Second World War. At that same time, the first signs of qualitative changes in the growth pattern could be observed. Presumably, it will be concluded that it was about 1945 when technical and economic life-spans ceased to be identical.

It is revealing to study the growth of the gross national product (GNP) in the USA during the twentieth century. Fixing the index at 100 in 1929 (i.e. immediately before the great Depression of the 1930s) a gradual increase can be noticed during the first three decades of the century, especially during the years immediately prior to 1920. The early 1930s are marked by recession, and the lowest index figures of 50–60 are reached in the middle of the 1930s. Then a change occurred, and from the middle of the 1930s the index curve rises more or less vertically, until the index for 1965 reaches approximately 550. The rapid growth of GNP in the 1940s and 1950s accompanied a noticeable growth in large companies. During this period it is as though the quantitative growth in production became the most significant sign of overall growth, not only for individual companies but for society as a whole. Growth, and more especially excessive growth, becomes a necessity for companies wishing to stand up to the two-fold pressure of falling prices and rising costs. Economic growth emerges as a fourth aim of social economy, alongside the three traditional aims of stable currency, constant high employment and a favourable balance of trade. Historically speaking, this is a new turn of events.

It is a situation in which all manufacturers (not only the largest and most dynamic, in highly technical spheres such as petrochemicals, applied electrotechnics, or drugs) are forced to invest an increasing proportion of their resources in specific research and development work. The effect of this new situation is felt in all fields of industry – even in such areas as heavy capital equipment where, until recently, radical changes in production methods and technology played a minor role in comparison with means of increasing productivity such as rationalisation, improved production-management and quality control. Should it prove possible to demonstrate that the importance of the technological life-span is now beginning to affect this sector, which lays claim to the main part of gross investments in industry, compelling evidence will have been discovered to indicate that the thesis formulated earlier is correct.

Such evidence does, indeed, seem to exist.

There are numerous indications, for example, that the period following the Second World War was of great significance and interest in this respect. From 1870 to 1890 the annual growth in production per worker in Swedish industry was negligible, a mere 0·7 per cent, due to constantly recurring crises such as in 1877 and 1890, increasing protectionism by means of corn laws which resulted in a reduction in earnings abroad, and structural problems in many branches of industry ("factory deaths"). Growth was noticeably greater in the years immediately preceding the First World War – 3·2 per cent on average – a phenomenon which may be related to increased international trade and a rapid growth of capital within industry itself. The inter-war period again shows a somewhat lower rate of growth – 2·9 per cent between 1921 and 1940 – which is chiefly explained by the international crisis of the period.

But then something happened.

Since 1946, production per worker has grown, on average, by almost 5 per cent annually – a rise which, because of the exponential character of the growth, is even more striking than that indicated by the difference between the 2·9 per cent of the inter-war years and the 4·7 per cent annually after 1946. Nor is this all, for if we analyse the way in which this growth in productivity has occurred, it becomes more and more apparent that the thesis is correct.

A specialist study of industry has been carried out, leading to results of particular significance in this kind of inductive argument. The technique factor (which can be defined as that production factor explaining growth in production unrelated to increased contributions by capital or workers) is divided into one part linked to investment and a remainder which reflects, among other things, the value of co-operation between the production factors and the quality of the labour force. The technique factor derived from investment quantifies such influences on increased production as the replacement of one unit of old capital by one new unit with higher productivity. In other words, given a specific quantity of capital and labour, organisational structure, etc. it is possible to increase production by replacing an old machine with a new one costing the same. The technique factor, linked to investment, increased industrial production by approximately 0·5 per cent annually between 1922 and 1939, and by an annual 1·2 per cent between 1947 and 1964. At the same time, the average annual production growth fell from 5·3 per cent to 4·3 per cent, implying that the significance for growth of the new capital rose from roughly 10 per cent between the wars to about 25 per cent in the period following 1947. The conclusion to be drawn is clear, that the amount of technical capital has increased in both periods, but at a much faster rate after the war than between the two wars.

In a study of industrial capital developments from 1940 to 1957, Erik Lundberg calculated the speed with which old capital was replaced in industry. He discovered that the average life-span for machines and buildings was thirty-three years, corresponding to a depreciation factor of 3 per cent. Other studies support this. Jan Wallander, for example, found that in Sweden in 1960 the average life-span for machine capital in industry was something over twenty-eight years. Åberg's study, which is the most recent (1969), deals with the period from 1947 to 1964 and indicates a depreciation rate of 2·7 per cent for machines and buildings combined; this corresponds to a life-span of almost forty years.

The really interesting feature in this analysis is the fact
that the post-war period differs so markedly from that
between 1922 and 1939; the average life-span, now forty
years, was then sixty years. One hypothesis is that the
replacement rate was constantly rising from 1922 to 1964,
and that this tendency was accentuated during the 1960s.
Expressed in another way, the investment-related technique
factor developed from a relatively minor influence on growth
into one of the most important, and the tendency was
especially marked during the 1960s. This hypothesis, in fact,
proves to be correct.

The investment-related technique factor of increased production grew rapidly between 1950 and 1970, and, as might
be expected, most noticeably towards the end of this period.
From 1950 to 1955, this part of the technique factor is
thought to have been responsible for approximately 0·7 per
cent of growth, but between 1966 and 1969 the percentage
rose to about 1·7. In other words, the growth of Swedish
industry in the 1960s can largely be explained as a result of
replacing an old technology by a new one. Old capital had to
be replaced with increasing speed, hence plants which were
physically perfectly usable were discarded or given less
important parts to play. In general, this latter practice meant
that equipment was not utilised to the full.

The suggestion that the economic wear of equipment in
use is a relatively new discovery for manufacturers can now
be seen as a reality, not merely a reasonable assumption.
That the degree of economic wear, rather than the technical
capacity of the plant, decides whether or not it must be
replaced, is a state of affairs which no longer applies only to
consumer goods but to major industrial equipment as well.
It should be possible to demonstrate this in any highly
developed industrial society with a capitalist economic
system: it is not a tendency restricted to Sweden alone.

The other suggestion, that the economic life-span is constantly decreasing, must also be considered proved on
equally good grounds. It provides an explanation, or at least

an indication, as to why the industrialised society is caught
in the "vicious circle of thinking in volume", with more and
more manufacturers being forced into a situation where they
must either invest or perish. Unless the investor makes a
really foolish decision, it always pays to invest, and the
dominant factor here is the question of resources. It is of
prime importance to secure the finance and the liquidity to
make the investment. The higher the saving proportionate
to resources, the better. The greater the proportion of the
credit and capital market which is ear-marked for industrial
investment, the greater the possibility for expansion and the
creation of a favourable external balance. From the viewpoint of social economy the investment quota must be
forced up – in 1870 the gross investments in Sweden constituted 8 per cent of the GNP, in 1970 a good 20 per cent.
However, that is not sufficient: if the GNP is to continue
rising in any highly industrialised country, it is essential that
the investment quota reaches the level of that in the growth
world's "pop idol", Japan. It is possible to find oases of
respite among the many areas of investment – sectors where
the capital is being used to the full before it is discarded.
However, expressed in simple terms, this means that an
industrialised society such as Sweden has embarked on a
course which, if taken to its ultimate conclusion, will make
new technology obsolete before it is even installed.

In his classical study, Walter Rostov divides economic
development into five stages of growth. The first is what
might be called the traditional society, in which science and
technology play a very small part, and the family and the
social class are the dominant institutions. Most of the population earn their living by agriculture, and production
methods are passed on from father to son. In the second
stage, societies begin to show some signs of change, such
as those seen in Western Europe in the seventeenth and
eighteenth centuries; people become aware of more economical methods of production, particularly in agriculture, and
certain industrial enterprises begin to emerge, notably the

textile industry. In the third stage, called the "take-off" by Rostov, economic growth is seen as a normal feature in the transformation of a society; industrialisation gets under way, and investment quotas begin to grow. In England the "take-off" period began at the end of the eighteenth century, in the USA and France in the middle of the nineteenth, and in Sweden after 1870. The fourth stage – development into the modern industrialised state – is characterised by constant economic changes, a rapid growth of international trade and so on. It has taken between fifty and seventy-five years from the beginning of the "take-off" for society to reach the stage of mature industrialisation. Finally comes the fifth stage, which Rostov calls "the age of mass consumption".

In certain respects Rostov's picture might well be a valuable instrument for analysis, but it is of little assistance in facilitating an understanding of a new phenomenon in the highly industrialised society of the twentieth century – the increasing interest in growth. Simply to say that we are now in "the age of mass consumption" tells us nothing. Although when seen in a historical perspective, a period of thirty to forty years is only a brief interval, it is long enough for anyone alive today to have great difficulty in realising what progress has been made during this time: from a stage when it was impossible, in any of the more important areas of society, to discard or functionally downgrade capital values as long as they worked properly, to a new age in which economic and technological life-spans no longer coincide. Furthermore, we have reached a position where not only perfectly functioning consumer items are thrown away and discarded, but technically faultless industrial capital equipment is scrapped and under-used. This is a qualitative change in the economic conditions of society which deserves a name of its own – the age of the economic life-span.

Chapter 3
The power of the possible

Regard for mankind itself and its fate must always be at the centre of technological ambitions. Never forget this in the midst of your diagrams and equations.

Albert Einstein

It is very important to saw off the branch on which we are sitting. For we have band saws which demand to improve their standards. Politics are sawing.

Herr Brunander
(*Grönköpings Veckoblad*)

The fact that economic wear appears to have assumed paramount significance in increasingly widespread fields of the investment sector should be a sufficiently interesting discovery on its own. However, a form of progress which persuades manufacturers (not just ordinary consumers) to discard material and probably also immaterial values with growing rapidity, despite the fact that they function perfectly well, implies certain consequences which require further consideration. The continuation of this process involves the wasting of scarce resources, the destruction of the environment and the creation of a society which many find intolerable, all at an ever-increasing rate. Demand is subordinated to supply in a highly undesirable way. For goods and services with an economic life-span shorter than their technological life-span, the ideal of progress rather than of need leads to a qualitatively new trend in the redirection of change, involving the replacement of existing production materials and the variety of products on offer at any given time.

Two essential questions remain unanswered. It seems that companies are irresistibly pressurised to introduce technological innovations. This can partly be explained by the management's drive and desire to expand, but in all probability it has wider implications. Our first task is to discover a pattern in the process which militates for technological change and results in firms finding it increasingly impossible to refrain from making, for instance, new investments until their old equipment is technically unserviceable. Moreover, it appears that innovation (i.e. the product of research, inventions and technological developments) is the decisive factor forcing progress upon them. It is, therefore, appropriate to study more closely the motivation of research workers, inventors and those employed on company development projects in their choice of research spheres.

The problem will be dealt with in this chapter by seeking to explain the forces working towards change in general, and towards the creation of new products in particular. We will also try to decide why progress does not autonomously move in the directions regarded by most people as reasonable and acceptable.

Possibly a new classification of products is required. "Producer goods" and "consumer goods", "non-durables" and "capital goods", or "everyday" and "luxury" articles are classifications intended to reflect differences in the purchaser's freedom of choice, the needs the product is intended to satisfy and the process by which it can effectively be distributed. A simple distinction between "replaceable goods" and "other goods" might be more suitable for the purposes of this discussion. "Capital goods" would be placed in the first category irrespective of whether they were producer or consumer capital goods, while of the non-durables, such items as clothes naturally fall into the "replaceable goods" classification. At a guess, the average Swedish consumer spends about 30 per cent of his net income on replaceable goods, the most characteristic feature of such articles being the fact that the decision to buy a new model or replace the old one tends to become increasingly dependent on forces beyond the user's control. More and more often, his decision seems to constitute formal confirmation of a change which has been initiated and fashioned elsewhere.

Developments determine demand to an increasing extent, rather than demand deciding developments as should be the case. All the activities in society which actually or apparently replace an existing product or service with a new model claiming to have a higher productivity, better capacity, etc., or to be more in keeping with present-day tastes and fashions, develop into some dynamic force which certain categories of consumer find difficult to resist and to which manufacturers are forced to adapt.

The power of economic life-span, or rather economic wear, obviously creates a symptomatic difficulty in investment calculations. The inaccuracy of such projections is indicated by the fact that their estimated profitability does not always coincide with the profitability actually achieved. Therefore, technicians sometimes manipulate the life-span in order to achieve the profitability which they intuitively believe to be there, and "unprofitable" investment decisions are either motivated by reference to qualitative advantages not shown in the calculations, or by introducing false solutions in the form of graphs showing the rate of obsolescence. The company *must* invest.

The explanation of this lies in the fact that the freedom of action enjoyed by individual manufacturers is severely limited by circumstances over which they have little or no immediate control. A company which is being forced to invest has not only been exposed to horizontal pressure from its competitors, but also – and this is the interesting feature – to vertical pressure originating in technological advances far removed from its own sphere of influence; it might be only a little more chromium plating, new packaging, mini-skirt turning into maxi-skirt, and so on.

The Sundsvall Bank is one of the few Swedish commercial banks which so far have not installed their own computers. For a number of years the bank has been utilising the Forestry Computer Centre, one of the major centres of its kind in Sweden, so has had frequent access to the most modern computers in the country.

In 1969 the directors of the Sundsvall Bank decided that its programme library should be modernised at a cost of several million kronor. Obviously, the bank already had a well-tried computer routine, but for various reasons it was felt that a re-organisation of the programme was necessary at that particular time. Calculations carried out to predict the profitability of the investment indicated that total expenditure would be reduced by between 300,000 and 400,000 kronor annually, if the volume of business remained constant, but that such a level of profitability could not be considered particularly high. Nevertheless, the directors and managers of the bank felt "forced" to make this investment, and it is here that the beginnings of an explanation become apparent. On account of its size, the Forestry Computer Centre had at an early stage acquired third generation computers, and owned two IBM 360/50 systems. This array gave the bank the opportunity to make use of the most advanced computer technology and equipment, comparable with that ordered by its major competitors.

Existing computer routines in the bank, however, were worked out for an older type of computer (IBM 1410), and so there was a gap between the services offered by the Computer Centre and those presupposed by the bank. This gap could have been bridged by "emulation techniques", which would simply entail the mechanical reprogramming of the IBM 1410 routines for the new computer, the IBM 360/50. However, this would have involved extra expense, and the bank felt the computer centre was hinting at increased charges and thus, implicitly or explicitly, exerting pressure. This seems to be the first element of vertical pressure.

Both the largest Swedish commercial banks, Svenska Handelsbanken and Skandinaviska Banken, had at that time earmarked considerable resources for the development of on-line systems. In practice this would mean that when a customer or bank official required the information, the state of a customer's account or his total commitments could be extracted immediately. In the long run it was possible to extend the system to include automatic cash dispensers and shop terminals, and one could imagine a society which would be totally independent of cash if such a project were put into operation. If the Sundsvall Bank, one of the major provincial banks, was to keep abreast with this development its library would have to be reprogrammed on purely technical grounds. Awareness of this produced significant horizontal pressure.

A critical point in the cycle of cause and effect must have been reached when the Forestry Computer Centre decided to replace its old equipment (IBM 1410), and it may well be that the situation facing the directors was not unlike that confronting the Sundsvall Bank. The manufacturers of the Centre's equipment, IBM, had developed third-generation computers and presumably made energetic efforts to sell them. It is reasonable to assume that just as the Bank faced increased costs as a result of wishing to continue with the old routine, so the Centre had to reckon with higher costs in its dealings with IBM in order to continue using the old equipment. This was the vertical pressure almost certainly experienced by the Forestry Centre, but horizontal pressure in the form of competition from competitors in the field was possibly even more powerful, presumably making the installation of more modern equipment necessary to safeguard its leading position among Swedish service centres.

A third stage in the chain of pressures can also be

envisaged, for even though IBM dominates 65–70 per cent of the total world computer market, it can be assumed that its competitors exerted considerable horizontal pressure. Should IBM fail to keep up with modern technology, it was obvious that a competitor would utilise the new techniques. Taking the argument one stage further and making hypothetical deductions from a rather diffuse situation, it might well be that the third-generation computers resulted from research into semiconductors and transistors which were superior to those previously available. It thus became possible to manufacture a product which needed less space, worked more quickly, had a higher capacity and could also be produced at a lower cost. Had IBM not followed in the footsteps of its competitors as soon as they began planning new products on the basis of these advances, it would probably have ceased being able to compete effectively. Like the Forestry Computer Centre and the Sundsvall Bank, IBM was presumably subjected to a combination of competitive and vertical pressures – the latter stemming from basic research and the manufacturers of components.

It seems, therefore, that the freedom of the individual manufacturer to choose his own pace in the field of technological developments is severely limited by decisions and actions carried out months or even years beforehand and well outside his own sphere of influence. With a little imagination it is possible to find a vertical chain of influences for virtually every disposable consumer product – cars, television sets, fashion goods and so on. However, this can also occur, to an increasing extent, with producer/capital goods and soft products in industry itself. Under the classical liberal doctrine, competition not only guaranteed effective production, but also ensured that only products with consumer appeal came onto the market. Because of his supremacy, the final user of the goods was the sole exerter of vertical pressure. That age now belongs to the distant past.

The driving force behind increased consumption and investment is no longer consumer demand and expressed need, but first and foremost pressure from below, from those deciding what the market shall be, from pseudo-improvements, and to an increasing extent from research and development. Competition has almost completely lost its function as the consumer's special emissary in questions relating to choice of products.

This situation has negative consequences in the sense that resources can fall short of the necessary increase in capital; that certain demands on production will be more than covered, while other equally desirable demands cannot be fulfilled; and that the external and internal environments will be negatively influenced. Thus the picture being built up indicates the possible areas, in a capitalist system, where it would be most practicable to take steps to control the situation. In a highly academic sense there are only two feasible solutions. Either the causes of upward pressure must be removed, which in the final analysis means restricting the activities carried out in the spheres of research and development within "acceptable" limits, and prohibiting all research and development work (as was suggested at a hearing of the US Senate's committee on the environment); or competition must be stopped.

These are extremely challenging conclusions. Not only to question technological development, but also to prescribe a monopoly seems to turn all traditional thinking upside-down. It is not, of course, realistic to take the conclusions to their logical limit, but the solution must be found somewhere along this path if we are to gain control. The upward pressure from technological developments gives a new dimension to competition, rarely mentioned in textbooks but presumably far more significant than competition based on price, service and quality, which has previously been the focus of attention. In the classic seventh chapter of his book *Capitalism, Socialism and Democracy*,[4] Joseph Schumpeter concentrates on showing that it is the competition from new products, new technology or new sources of supply which is of real importance. Technological developments, he maintains, are like an industrial mutation process which constantly revolutionises the economic structure from inside, and ceaselessly destroys the old for the purpose of creating new forms. In his opinion, this process of generating destruction is the essence of capitalism.

Yet this dynamic quality in the structure is not the complete answer. The question still remains as to why the research carried out and the constant discovery of new methods fail to produce skills and technology which are not only meaningful but important to most people. It is fair to ask why an inferior product is so frequently foisted upon us when it is clear that something far better and equally profitable could easily have been manufactured. The conclusion must be that there is some mechanism of choice parallel to and superior to the management, which is guided not by rationality but by circumstances and chance. This autonomous process can only be revealed by closely examining the criteria by which the research worker, the inventor and the development section choose their fields of activity. The working hypothesis is the existence of a common pattern of choice of areas of activity for all fields of development, from basic research outside the company to the applied development of products within the company itself.

What determines research?

It is logical to begin with the fundamental assumptions of research and to base this part of the analysis primarily on the book which, as C. P. Snow points out, gives the clearest impression of the way in which creative research is carried out. In *Double Helix*,[5] James D. Watson, the biologist and Nobel Prize winner, gives a day-to-day account of the determination of the structure of the DNA molecule – the discovery which led to an understanding of the way in which genetic information is governed in virtually all living organisms, high and low alike.

Watson makes it perfectly obvious that the research project was not successfully concluded without friction, difficulties and mistakes. While in Europe on a research fellowship, he clashed with the authorities administering the fellowship, because they would not allow him to work in the institution which he considered most suitable. Francis Crick, with whom Watson shared the Nobel Prize for medicine in 1962, was considered a theoretically brilliant man, full of good ideas, yet was regarded as something of a failure. At the age of thirty-five he had still not completed his doctorate, and he was a constant source of irritation to the Principal of the Institution, Sir Lawrence Bragg. In 1951 Crick and Watson, believing that they had determined the structure of the DNA molecule, invited a number of colleagues to examine the discovery. However, it was decided that the solution was not sufficiently well-founded, and as a result, Bragg refused permission for any further work on DNA to be carried out. Crick was sent back to work on the thesis for his doctorate, and Watson to work on tobacco mosaic virus (TMV). However, a vital component in TMV was nucleic acid, "and so it was the perfect front to mask my continued interest in DNA". How the structure of DNA – the double helix – was discovered is also the story of how theory and experiment were significantly linked. Francis Crick was responsible for building the mathematical model, and was therefore the first to be able to demonstrate the molecule's helical shape. The results were later confirmed experimentally by means of X-ray crystallography and, at the same time, the construction of the three dimensional model clearly determined the appearance of the molecule.

In this connection, the case of Linus Pauling – undoubtedly the most outstanding figure in the field, and also Crick and Watson's greatest rival – is of interest for several reasons. In 1951 Pauling had discovered the structure of what is known as the "alfa helix", and to their great surprise Crick and Watson were forced to admit that his result was a product of commonsense and reason rather than the fruits

of complicated mathematical juggling. Some equations did
enter Pauling's argument, but in most cases words alone
would have sufficed. Instead of pen and paper, his main
tools were some molecular models, resembling the toys
found in nursery schools. As Watson points out, only a
genius of Pauling's calibre could have achieved the correct
result by playing like a ten-year-old. This kind of insight
was extensively employed by Crick and Watson, who
also spent a great deal of time with "toys". On one occasion
when they were sure that their conclusions were virtually
one hundred per cent correct, they spent several days trying
to determine the relative positions of the atoms with the
help of plumb lines and measuring sticks, instruments not
normally used in basic research.

This discovery was thus the result of a happy combination
of theory, experiment and model-building, with an element
of chance. Many mistakes were made, much of the research
was unsystematic and much was due to luck. For instance,
one of the world's foremost organic chemists, Jerry
Donohue, also worked at the institute. "The unforeseen
dividend of having Jerry share an office with Francis, Peter
and me, although obvious to all, was not spoken about. If he
had not been with us in Cambridge, I might still have been
pumping for a like-with-like structure." At that time they
had been following the wrong track altogether.

The international character of basic research, the severe
competition between different groups of research workers,
the difficulties and coincidences which influence both the
results and the approach, the need for inter-disciplinary
contacts and work on different levels – these are typical and
well-known factors which are emphasised and exemplified in
Watson's book.

However, it is also made clear – and this is the important
point – that the basic researcher's choice of his sphere of
study is not determined by a systematic and conscious
analysis of need or demand, but rather by coincidence, his
own inclinations, and access to technical resources and

interested colleagues. Did Crick and Watson ever discuss the consequences of their work, except in general terms such as how it would be the "discovery of the century"? Judging by the book, the answer is "No". The sancrosanct liberal conviction that an unhindered search for knowledge is a matter of the highest intrinsic value, ultimately leads to a situation in which it is considered unreasonable even to question the utility of such a pursuit.

Are there any common factors between a successful scientific discovery on the one hand, and an innovation (whether a discovery or the result of systematic industrial development work) on the other? That this seems likely is borne out by Arvid Palmgren, the legendary development manager of SKF in its early years, who believes that one of the most important aspects of a work of invention is to discover all the parallel approaches to the solution of a problem.

> "If a single one is missed, it is not unthinkable that precisely that approach was the best, and the most suited to further development. In order to create a product of real and lasting economic value it is not necessary merely to be sure that it is an acceptable solution to the problem, but also, by means of experiment, to convince oneself that no other more or less similar solutions can be found which have anything like the same economic value."

If the word "economic" is replaced by "scientific" the commentary is as valid for basic research work as for invention, and Crick and Watson followed the advice which Palmgren gave to inventors.

Functional reliability seems to be a characteristic of successful inventions; James Watt's steam engine was a functionally reliable variation on an earlier discovery. Originality is another characteristic feature of success; the tetrahedron as a container is an original and radical solution, and what is known as the Lindén crane is another example. The requirements which Elis Lindén sought in his crane were that it should be able to reach any part of a building, that it should be possible to increase its height as the building went up, and that it should be capable of remote control. The first condition was met by placing the crane in the centre of the building (at the same time making the use of a shorter arm feasible), and this also solved the problem of increasing its height as building progressed. Remote control was not a particularly complicated technical problem. In comparison with other alternatives on the market, most of which were restricted to running on tracks, the Lindén crane was a radical, original solution to a problem.

Good timing also seems to be a fundamental condition for the success of a new venture. The actual timing is often decisive for the success of scientific work and in the sphere of practical inventions, since certain theoretical and experimental data must be known before the new product can be made. An example is the particularly serious difficulty experienced by SKF in the further development of roller bearings; it appears that when they were developing these around 1920, the only theoretical base lines upon which they could work – the so-called theories of elasticity dating from about 1880 – were neither sufficient in themselves nor adaptable for working out the stress on the material, the durability or the strength of the new bearings.

A further important time factor is connected with the market conditions available for the new technology. For instance, in order to fully understand the reasons for the exceptional attention attracted by C. E. Johansson's gauge blocks, the extensive use made of them, and also the speed with which they came to dominate the market, one must appreciate the significance of the time at which they were developed. Cheap steel, machine tools, the beginning of standardisation, the assembly line, together with electricity and the growth of automation, were the most important components in the technology of the new mass production. The demand for manufacturing precision was a logical consequence.

Within less than twenty-five years after 1856 came three inventions which revolutionised steel production – the Bessemer, Martin and Thomas processes. The availability of cheap steel naturally led to a demand for machinery to process it, but the commonest types of machine tools – lathes, cutters and drills – had mainly been developed on the basis of completely different conditions. Thus, after 1870, production machinery was also developed according to entirely new principles. For instance, weapons were manufactured by first constructing machines to make each separate part. By making identical components of all the types needed, weapons could be mass-produced, and precision in manufacturing was essential for the parts to be interchangeable.

C. E. Johansson's tool has to be viewed with this development in mind. Towards the end of the nineteenth century, "measurement blocks" began to be used as part of industrial production and to check the final product (quite apart from the customary instruments for measuring and checking). The steel blocks were furnished with parallel blades for measurement, the distance between these blades representing the required size. One block was constructed for each size or, occasionally, made with "steps" so that it was possible to use the same piece of steel for a variety of measurements. Previously, any weapon manufacturer (or any other manufacturer using standardised long series production methods) needed a very large number of blocks, and often had to construct an entirely new jig every time changes in pattern were made, which was both costly and time-consuming. What C. E. Johansson did was to develop a combination system which radically reduced the number of blocks needed; in addition these were made with greater precision than before.

While invention is the country cousin of basic research, it can be maintained that production development is an even more mundane occupation. Nevertheless, the number of features which they have in common is striking. A study of

production development in a factory shows that the choice
of research is often the result of an opportunity which
suddenly presents itself, or of a coincidence; while advances
are largely based on previous knowledge and the availability
of resources, they may also depend on chance circumstances; that difficulties and mistakes are common; and that
the reward – the ability of the new technology to create new
income – seems to be linked to the timing, quality and
efficiency of the new product rather than to the area of
application.

One reason for the initiation of new ventures is that the
development department of a large firm may press for a
change. Another might be that the firm is doing badly, or
conversely that it is doing well, or that a supplier or
customer suggests a new approach. The choice of product is
often, but not always, linked with some sort of initiative.
The particular direction taken by some development work
might well have been decided by a customer expressing
some specific wish, although judging by the small number of
empirical studies on this subject, such a situation must be
remarkably rare. Need is one of many factors influencing the
choice of product, but it is by no means the most important.

It is quite logical that the impetus to manufacture new
products should, in the first instance, come from contacts
with other firms working in the same field, either at home or
abroad. On the one hand, companies can best discuss technical problems with others working along similar lines; on
the other, it is obvious that only within their own sphere can
they expect to find ideas for new initiatives which are
workable given the staff and the production resources available to them. The fact that profitability increases with the
level of technology (as several empirical studies have shown)
can be expressed more accurately by saying that profitability
increases with the improved performance, efficiency and
quality of a product. Therefore, it is reasonable to assume
that all manufacturers have an innate tendency to search for
new high-level products in basic research, the work of

inventors and, more frequently, through contacts with highly developed technology in their own field.

Companies can be divided into three categories, depending on their level of technology. The first type leads in its field, in both technology and application, and is thus in close contact with basic research and inventors who have something to offer. Such companies allocate substantial resources to their own development work. The second category, whose profitability is often outstandingly high, seeks co-operation with some of the technological leaders, often on the basis of manufacturing licences. These firms might carry out their own development work, but in many cases this appears to be marginal in nature, or else aimed at adapting to the market. The third group consists of manufacturers who are not only on a technologically lower level, but whose financial situation is usually far less satisfactory. From this it follows that the organisational pressures for new developments and changes within such companies are of a completely different nature from those operating in the first two categories. It has also been shown, as might be expected, that firms of the third type produce goods which are the most radically different compared with those already on the market.

In recent years, a large Swedish manufacturer of heavy equipment has made certain new types of hydraulic crane for use on ships. The reason for the firm's concentration on this area is interesting when seen against the background just outlined. In the 1950s one of the owners, who was technical director and therefore responsible for the firm's development work, met a private inventor who had developed a hydraulic engine. Impressed by the possibilities of hydraulic techniques, he bought the rights, and soon afterwards the company realised that ships' cranes were a likely field in which to apply the new engine.

In a nutshell, the pattern was one of an intelligent and imaginative director who was fortunate enough to come into contact with an inventor able to offer him an embryonic product, which was more or less suited to the firm's financial resources, and required no more than a reasonable degree of innovation. It is worth noting that only after the company had acquired the development rights was it possible to decide on the market to which the invention could be applied.

The characteristics of innovation

It is noticeable that certain categories keep reappearing in accounts of how basic research is effected, how inventors work, or how firms decide on the development of their products. "Coincidence", "circumstances", "chance", "good luck" and perhaps even "Divine Providence" are words found time after time. Pure coincidence gave James Watson the opportunity to hear Maurice Wilkens in Naples in the spring of 1951. From this came the realisation that genes can be crystallised, leading him to deduce that they must have a regular construction which it should be possible to discover. This started a chain of events which culminated in the establishment of the structure of the DNA molecule a little over a year later. A coincidence which was almost a mistake led to the discovery of the strength of aluminium and iron alloy, the basis on which the Swedish firm of Kanthal was founded. Tetra Pak packaging was given its form, and consequently its name, by pure chance.

Is this really a discernible pattern, or merely a product of an unfortunate choice of examples, or a false interpretation? Do chance, coincidence, circumstance, opportunity, or even neglect and indifference really play such large parts in the development process? If this is the case, it hardly seems to coincide with the picture of order and thoroughness, well-planned work, clarity of thought, and generally systematic actions which we like to ascribe to scientists and managers. However, although the opposite of what we might expect, it is not mere fiction but a reality, which in practice is readily understandable as the logical consequence of the most characteristic feature of the innovation process – the power of the possible.

Whether or not a scientific discovery is an innovation very much depends on the definition used. Innovation normally implies adaptation, function and need, rather than knowledge and basic research, and it is usually employed when referring to technological, financial, and administrative changes within a form or an organisation. Nevertheless, in the sense that – in principle – all the qualities of a discovery emanate from a successful innovation, a discovery can also be said to *be* an innovation.

Starting from the premise that an innovation is a radical change which is new to the relevant milieu, it is also the synthesis of a number of possibilities such as theory, technology, market resources and so on, and is thus the visible result of a chain of developments – the innovation process. This includes all the toil, effort, opposition, resources, time, etc. necessary to produce a concrete innovation from basic research and development work. The process begins with the initiation and ends with the introduction and acceptance of a new product. The initiation can be an idea, a mathematical discovery or an invention, but equally well it can be a plentiful supply of money, a lack of money, a change in the law or a customer enquiry. Change is naturally a vague term in itself, but in this connection it is used to refer to a radical change which has come into use and been accepted; this is perhaps the most important distinction between innovation and change of any kind. It might be a verified scientific achievement or a product accepted by the market, but it could just as well be a manufacturing process or a new routine which has been put into production or adapted to use. It is then reasonable to define the other limit of the innovation process, which is simply the dissemination of an innovation; here we enter the sphere which Joseph Schumpeter defined as "imitation", and which others have called "diffusion".

Perhaps the concepts of innovation and the innovation

process are best understood by imagining a vast number of possibilities, a well of potential from which certain phenomena are tapped. Some are viable, and are recognised as innovations. Others are not so successful and are seen merely as ideas, projects, sketches, or completely without substance. Therefore, any innovation can be considered as the synthesis of a number of possibilities, the process being the successful attempt to add something, at present lacking, to existing ingredients – some further unique piece of knowledge, newly discovered interrelationship, new perspective and so on. It is not unlike the building of a radically new structure of possibilities: sometimes not all the materials needed are to hand; sometimes the money required to finance the project is not available; sometimes no one wants to live in it when it is finally built; sometimes no one knows what it should look like or where it should be situated. But, occasionally, the project is crowned with success. The innovation is the result of a fortunate set of circumstances.

What is striking is the continuity, the fact that the innovation process is so clearly influenced by previous events which are often in the quite distant past. If component A and component B are available, component C results; this logically leads to component D which comes into being, quite literally, whether we want it or not. If one person chooses to ignore it, someone else will take it up. Scientific, technological, and industrial developments become an inexorable process once the foundations have been laid. In this respect we can rest assured that something will happen sooner or later; it is only a question of time. This realisation emphasises the absurdity of placing the individuals – whether scientists, inventors or industrialists – on a pedestal. The Nobel Prize, in fact, should be seen as an anachronism in this context.

Thus change, progress and innovations all find their substance in a well of possibilities amongst components consisting of knowledge, theory, technology, energy, monetary resources, markets, etc. These raw materials can be

combined in an infinite variety of ways, and from this well a
constant stream of new results can be tapped in a process of
innovation. Some people and firms are more clever than
others – these become the legendary research workers, inventors and successful companies.

What benefit do we derive from this analysis? In what ways
has it helped us to understand the causes of uncontrolled
technological development?

It has been demonstrated that in an advanced industrial
society, manufacturers are increasingly forced into decisions
resulting in perfectly usable capital equipment being
scrapped or under-utilised. The reason for this is to be
found in the simple rule which guides them: "if we do not
innovate someone else will, and this will diminish our
competitiveness". In a market economy, manufacturers can
never afford to lose time, and there is no refuge where they
can pause in their efforts to develop and exploit a more
effective technology. The most important thing to remember
is that this situation is due to the structure of a capitalist
economic system, where there are a great many decision-
making units which, while closely linked to and dependent
on each other, are unable to influence either each other or
the source of the pressures, the knowledge and the technology which constantly militate for change.

The power of the possible does not give necessity a
privileged position, and there is one feature of progress
which is particularly thought-provoking. The reward to the
scientist, inventor or manufacturer for a successful innovation – whether measured in terms of profitability, fame or
general respect – seems to be proportional to the degree of
efficiency, originality, good design, timing, general validity,
precision, etc. of his innovation. In short, it is essentially
connected to short-term characteristics. It is easier to point
to aspects which are apparently without significance for

progress, such as the use to which the object may be put, and its possible consequences.

This last remark does not, of course, imply that the extent of the field to which some invention can be applied is without any significance for its development. It is rather that, since the choice of a field is clearly determined by outside influences and available resources, the reward for a specific manufacturer in a specific situation is likely to be linked more closely to such characteristics of a product as its efficiency, appearance, price and so on than to its future function.

This analysis should give cause for reflection on at least one point. It seems to indicate that the irresistible dynamism of the capitalist system – and therefore its tendency to get out of control – is related to its structure and mode of functioning rather than to the people running it and working within its framework.

Before this observation is expanded in Chapter 5, another fundamental topic must be examined – that of the defective system of value measurements in industrialised society.

Continuity and the influence of circumstances are two aspects of this topic in that they are signs of the power of the possible. Changes do not, on the whole, result from criticism or dislike of what we already have, but rather as an outcome of new possibilities. The decisive factor is not the *impossibility* of accepting something, but rather the *possibility* of doing something else. The obvious conclusion, which seems trivial and therefore goes unnoticed, is that the result is always subordinate to the possibility. This means that if we cannot control the possibilities – and we are unable to do so at the moment – we cannot expect to control further developments.

Chapter 4
What is a manufacturing firm?

Misfortune must be looked at from all angles
for from the right it looks straightforward and from the
left like progress
and from behind like consideration
and from in front like advantage and progress
and from above and below it seems to have feet and a head.
Misfortune must be looked at from all angles
If you are lucky you will then notice:
it is misfortune.

Erich Fried

To put it briefly, it is impossible to define a manufacturing firm precisely. No manager exists who can define the borderline between his organisation and the world around it – not if he expects to have his definition accepted by others. The most we can strive for is to give as good a description as possible, though this will inevitably be incomplete, and we can assume that such descriptions of manufacturing firms as we have – scheme of organisation, account sheet, calculations of profit and loss, etc. – are far from fulfilling even this ambition. The point is that the picture which almost everyone forms when thinking of a manufacturing company is bound to be based on out-of-date information, incomplete details and a one-sided account of the facts.

The weaknesses of such descriptions are, predictably, so marked that it is necessary to classify their faults. One way of doing this is to query when, how and by whom the description was made, and it is also important to enquire for what purpose it was written. The picture drawn can only be judged for quality and limitations if something is known of the time to which it is applicable, the person who initiated it, and the comprehensiveness of the data used.

It would be oversimplification to say that, on the whole, the same criteria of validity apply to combinations of words and figures – normally called facts, data or information – as to the most sophisticated aggregates of concepts and symbols. They are all abstractions, pictures of real, tangible things and situations. The distinction between the *structure* of this picture (routine, technology, computing, etc.) and its *contents* (e.g. current data) is something that need not concern us, for the simple reason that the important feature on which we should concentrate is the picture's relative ability to describe or guide in a given situation. We are not interested in how this is achieved. In general the chief demand can be defined as the need for the information provided by the picture to be as up-to-date, complete and impartial as the task and situation permit.

The influence of time

Hegel maintained that every definition of time contains contradictions. In formal logic, the basic premise is simple enough: that A is A, and everything is identical with itself. However, Hegel believed this to be impossible. His definition of existence as a living organic unity of constantly changing elements is fundamental. The conclusion of his reasoning is, quite simply, that a description of an organisation or manufacturing firm, for example, is inaccurate if we fail to take into account the fact that the organisation will not be the same at the point in time t_1 as it is at time t_2.

This is in itself a trivial observation, which nevertheless represents an important insight. A plan of an organisation in this perspective becomes a more or less worthless image of reality. It has been suggested instead that the description of a company should take the form of a "mobile" in which the structure and connections are constantly changing position and content.

The time relationship becomes even more important when the picture is not only used to give an impression of the organisational structure, or a balance account, but also to study the methods of controlling and running a company. The use of operational analytical methods for the examination of production techniques is one example. From the models available, one is chosen which looks as though it will more or less fit (M_1); with a little luck this will become what the systems analysts call a "homomorphism of reality", a model containing certain characteristic features of reality as it was at a certain point in time.

The next step is to register how reality behaves, and here some simplification is necessary so that the borderlines between the various parts of the model can be clearly defined. Exceptions cannot be taken into account. All this takes time, but the description (M_2) which gradually emerges on the basis of the model (M_1) is true of reality (R_1). However, reality has since changed to R_2.

On the basis of M_2 it is necessary to manage and direct. The tasks implied by M_2 are, however, only based on a fraction of its potential informative capacity – the fraction which we have succeeded in gathering and arranging since M_1 was created. Thus, the information available for deciding on management principles is based on the still further reduced and simplified model (M_3). However, M_3 is also based on our concept of R_1, but reality has now changed to R_3, etc.

This problem of obsolete facts and descriptions is obviously encountered in other guises. For instance, it was discovered that the accounts received by a commercial bank from its commercial customers (presumably an important source of information in judging creditworthiness) were, on average, passed on to the bank seven months after the end of the accounting year. Inevitably the information was out of date by the time of the annual review. Add to this the delay before the bank received the material and the time taken for it to be analysed, and it is obvious that the picture of reality (i.e. of the firm) emerging, in which the bank is particularly interested (information on liquidity, length of order books, etc.) is, in fact, no longer a true representation of the situation, and consequently almost useless. In a situation like this it is quite understandable, and perfectly ethical, that the banker's favourite means of gleaning information is so solidly based on personal contacts, second-hand information, visits to the companies concerned, hearsay and rumour. Stafford Beer sometimes disturbs his listeners by insisting that the measures and initiatives of economic policy carried out by the British government are consistently wrong, since they are out of touch with movements in economic reality – the very factors which they aim at stabilising but which, instead, they end up by accentuating. The methods employed to tackle such problems as unemployment, economic stagnation or housing shortages are characterised by our attempts to treat symptoms without first understanding the illness which produces them. Reality is so extremely complex that conventional methods give us no opportunity to undertstand how it works or to appreciate the importance of making the right decisions *at the right time*. It is as though we were pulling at different loose ends, consequently only making the situation worse.

The incomplete balance sheet

The next problem is to define the degree of accuracy and completeness and the extent of agreement between model and reality.

Everything indicates that the traditional specification of assets employed in estimating balances is unsatisfactory. It is appreciated that the company's physical assets such as machines, inventories, stores, outstanding debts and so on cannot be estimated exactly in the balance sheets, since important data are missing. The firm which has a considerable store of knowledge, better routines, and is more ready to adapt, or even attracts a greater degree of customer loyalty, has a larger potential and therefore more accessible resources in the broad sense of the term, though an outside assessor would be unable to judge the value of this advantage. It seems absurd that whereas an office chair is assigned a certain value in a balance sheet, the skill, loyalty or motivation of the person who occupies it, all of which are infinitely more valuable to the company, are not taken into account. It is a mystery that a firm which is is prepared to list its assets on a balance sheet "to the nearest pound", should be aware that perhaps half its assets are not even mentioned. The demand for precision, made by double-entry book-keeping must naturally be satisfied and respected, but the next step from this – to present the world at large with, for instance, a balance sheet estimating assets at £119.000.46 – is a considerable one.

The balance sheet is exclusively a quantitative statement of assets (and debts), but even so not all "quantities" are included. The qualitative aspect does not appear at all. The quality of the physical capital, such as the strategic value of a company's stocks or the technical level of its "know-how", is completely ignored. The quality of the work-force, including their training, loyalty and so on, is something intangible about which no statement can be made. The quality of the organisation and its potential, irrespective of physical assets and the disposition of staff, is also ignored. Because research and development are not tied to specific persons and have not been given concrete expression in "capital" it is impossible to comment on these aspects which nevertheless are of such importance for the company's future viability. Nor is

anything known of the organisation's ability to choose new
objectives or to change the basis of its operations, about the
image of its products or the loyalty of its customers.

The calculations of cost and income used, whether called
"prime cost calculations" or "marginal cost calculations",
are as incomplete as the balance sheet. As a first step,
deductions are made from income to cover tangible labour
and material costs, and then for recurrent expenses dictated
by the organisation, followed by extraordinary financial
expenses, etc., as far as the object of the calculations necessitates. It is easier and more interesting to list the uses of
resources to which no reference is made. Certain assets, such
as clean air and fresh water, are used without cost (or at least
have been until recently). The cost of any deterioration in a
firm's labour relations has never been measured. Solidarity
within the company can lead to putting up with cost-
reducing measures which may appear positive on the basis
of present calculation methods but which in reality are
negative steps guaranteeing a rise in future costs. Failure to
make a particular investment might seem like a saving, but
on closer examination it could well turn out to be an
invisible expense which has to be borne sooner or later. A
relative degeneration of the quality of physical assets is
always costly, but is never included in the calculations
where it ought to appear. While such items as a qualitative
reduction in the technological level of fixed capital assets,
failure to make a replacement or to reduce a current value
(the quantitative quality) of unusable (qualitative) stores or
stocks, are obviously items of expenditure, they are seldom
assessed when changes occur. If a company reduces expenditure by means of a relative lowering of its quality levels,
this will mean a short-term financial gain, but in the long
run it will have to be paid for.

It is worth looking at this philosophy from another viewpoint. There are certain tangible costs and regular extra
expenses which are usually ascribed to a specific product, in
addition to a share of the total expenditure; in other words it

is given a price which, in accounting terms, reflects its cost
to the firm. However, it seems fairly certain that this is an
unsatisfactory method of calculating, partly for the reasons
just stated and partly because it completely ignores any
expenditure on this product outside the company. Instead,
these costs and expenses are placed elsewhere – on society,
on the consumer, or on the employees. Ideally, each product
should bear all its own costs "from the cradle to the grave",
including true costs for the use of such scarce resources as
water and air, not only raw materials. Other items which
should be taken into consideration are development and
production costs, distribution and service charges, social
costs associated with use, and finally destruction and re-cycling costs. This does not happen in practice today, and
perhaps it never will. However, it is possible that different
forms of technical assessment could help us.

The balance sheet's specification of assets, and the profit
and loss assessment's cost specification are, each in its own
way, unsatisfactory statements. It must be as difficult for a
potential purchaser to assess the value of a company in
which he is interested, as it is for any other person or
organisation needing to assess the firm. It will be difficult for
the directors and owners to decide what really represents a
saving, and what is merely the postponement of some
inevitable expenditure which will be greater when it finally
comes. Furthermore, it will be difficult, if not impossible,
for professional representatives to assess the way in which
the management of a firm carries on its business. The
current method, whereby the effectiveness of a company is
judged purely on an analysis of variable results such as
profit, productivity, costs, etc., might well lead to disadvan-
tageous methods of running a firm. Converting important
human assets into cash resources is one of our commonest
means of rationalisation.

Even if a change of approach were theoretically desirable,
it could never be carried out in reality, for it is impossible to
change qualitative reputations into pounds and pence. One

of the two main objections is that the formulation of theory is now so advanced that it can only be a question of a few years before we are able to keep accounts of such human assets as the value of the staff employed. At the same time, it is perfectly possible to mix quantitative information with qualitative. The difficulty is that part-interests from various quarters, both inside and outside the organisation, will militate against a comprehensive account of qualitative changes.

The image seen through one man's eyes

Finally, the comprehensiveness of the image is an important but often overlooked aspect of all descriptions. Expanding Hegel's arguments on identity, it is possible to say that the picture of an organisation at a certain point in time (t_n) has no specific identity unless we simultaneously relate this to the person responsible for it.

We talk of Volvo as though Volvo existed in an unambiguous and generally accepted sense, yet Volvo as a comprehensive concept, and thus as "objective" reality, naturally does not exist. All that does exist is a personal concept of Volvo; the concept in the thoughts of the viewer, or in the picture presented. There are as many abstractions of the reality of Volvo as there are observers; Volvo $_1$ is not the same as Volvo $_2$.

Supposing we could visualise a manufacturing company as an objective reality, something existing in a well-defined form in the real world. Imagine that we then gave some individual, unconnected with the firm, the task of describing what he saw. If he were to give an all-round picture, he would place himself, as it were, on an imaginary movable platform and view it from a certain angle. From this point he would portray the firm from above, below, the side and so on, and several images would emerge. It is certain that none would be unambiguous or complete. If, as a second step,

this observer was replaced with another, a new set of
descriptions would result which would be just as imperfect,
having the same lack of unity, and equally dependent on the
platform's specific position. This is a simple analogy, but it
does serve to indicate the limitations of present descriptive
methods.

The first weakness in the method is that we do not usually
declare *who* has written the description. The portrait bears
the signature of the painter, whether visibly or not, and
reflects his training, knowledge, preferences and evaluations,
whether these are his own or merely acquired. We are not
seeking the name of the person, but rather what he stands
for and whom he represents.

The preconceptions regarding work, and the framework
of the ideas of the quantitative viewer, especially the
mathematician, merit further discussion. In recent years
mathematical and statistical methods have been used to an
increasing extent; this emanates from the military and strategic
calculations concerning logistics and quality control which
were carried out during the Second World War. The areas
to which these methods have been adapted have extended
from the traditional science-related fields to national economy, sociology, psychology, language, etc., and most important of all to industrial economy by means of operational
analysis. This latter development mainly occurred during
the 1960s.

The difficulty with quantitative models, apart from the
language problem, is to be sought in the *apparent*
objectivity, or lack of bias in mathematical presentation.
Mathematicians are thought to be free from human feelings,
the understandable but incorrect assumption being that the
precision of the description implies the objectivity of the
result. However, this supposition ignores the basis on which
the description was formulated and, in fact, one of our
commonest misconceptions is the idea that a mathematician's work is free from subjective evaluations. In reality,
there are few scientists whose work equals in subjectivity

and value judgements the work of mathematicians, statisticians and operations analysts. It is not so much the conclusions that are at fault as the theoretical basis from which they start – their choice of analytical instruments. The store of theories to which a mathematician has access is severely limited both by the constant development of theory and, more generally, by the analyst's own training and experience. This is particularly obvious when his methods are adapted to economic, political, and social problems in which the degree of complexity is noticeably higher than in many scientific fields. It is safe to conclude that straight lines are much more common in the model-builder's workshop than in the reality he is trying to describe.

The second difficulty with present methods is that only one line of approach is used in a description. When describing an organisation from above – particularly when speaking of the impression given to outsiders – it follows that the model presented is the one which the management wishes to be seen. In other words, the platform has been fixed at a definite angle. An annual statement to the press (probably written by the managing director, with the assistance of an economic adviser and the director's assistant), might tell of increased turnover, a favourable cost trend, or the highest net profit yet made. However, this is not necessarily the true picture. If the employees were allowed to write an annual report, it would be able to complement, clarify, perhaps even refute the official – and favourable – report on the firm's activities in a variety of ways: the pressure of lowering costs has created unrest in the organisation; staff turnover is higher than usual in this branch; the morale index (a technical possibility) is at its lowest for five years; the firm's long-term planning has been limited, and investments in new developments reduced, etc.

How is it that the material on which our conception of a firm is based is always so one-sided? Is this just a left-over from the days when the owner's dominant role made it patently clear that an outsider's view of the firm must be entirely fashioned firstly by the contractors and later by directors? The answer is probably not so simple.

Paradoxically enough, an outsider's view of a company was probably nearer the truth fifty years ago than it is now. An annual report from 1920 would contain a statement of accounts and a calculation of profit and loss just as in the present day, with no mention of stocks and other hidden assets. It is not a question of more details being given then than now, but that the world described was more strictly quantifiable in financial terms than is the case today. Any assets, in the broadest sense of the term, which were omitted from the balance sheet were relatively less important than in the present-day situation, and the distinction between chance $_1$ and chance $_2$ was less in 1920 than in 1970. The total store of knowledge in a firm, or the company's ability to adapt – factors not shown in a balance sheet – are relatively more decisive today than fifty years ago.

Perhaps this indicates that over a long period we have moved away from a dualistic, static, concrete, and therefore relatively unambiguous and well-ordered business world, towards one which is far more pluralistic, dynamic, abstract and consequently ambiguous and richly varied. Formerly, there was not so much to discuss.

At the same time it is disconcerting that, in many ways, we seem still to be living in a world which went out of existence long ago. Certain forces in a company are thoughtlessly credited with influence and a degree of attention which is disproportionate to their importance today, and merely reflects the role they have played in the past. According to Ernest Thiel in his memoirs, a bank's structure rests on a few fundamental cornerstones. One of these is high liquidity, and another is an unexhausted issue credit (by which he means the financial support which the shareholders are prepared to accept). "In fact such an army of shareholders is one of a banker's most valuable assets, and he must make great efforts to keep them." This sort of attitude, however, belongs to history.

New issues are less important for the financing of a company today; in most cases there is no longer any reason to heed such statements as, "We must retain the confidence of our shareholders, for we might get into the situation in which we have need of their financial support." Such statements suggest that the possibility of issuing new shares in order to gain access to capital is still an important factor, something which hardly coincides with the facts. If we analyse the Swedish credit and capital market from 1963-9 (i.e. the lending of credit institutions, the amount of long-term capital made available and – particularly interesting in the present context – the size of new issues), we find that the shareholders only account for an average of 5 per cent of the total financial resources added to business and industrial life from outside. It is reasonable to conclude that their share in the total contribution to new funds is diminishing.

Modern trends thus give the shareholder a decreasingly important part to play. Neither the directors, the management, nor even the shareholders' own organ – the General Meeting – pay him anything more than symbolic attention. This is a completely logical and foreseeable development, yet for some reason an important group of business analysts – the business editors – apparently focus their interest on him as much as ever. Their terms and concepts are still tied closely to the shareholder in respect of share dividends and so on, and their presentation is mainly aimed at passing on information which can be of specific use to those holding shares in a company.

The business editor's unique position – characterised by independence, an analytical capacity, and great drive – should be put to better use. His bias towards the shareholder should be replaced by a more general approach in which the interests of customers, society, and employees are all considered and commented on.

A company's field of activities is hedged in by society, employees, customers, owners, etc., and if a true picture is to be established, the company must be viewed from more than one vantage point. To maintain that it is possible to see everything from one angle alone may be suspect, but it seems to be the most common approach today. In general, it is easiest to rely on what is customary and readily available: the use of models and methods of describing phenomena are no exception to this. However, the models we have in stock are based on traditional methods, and might therefore give out-of-date, incomplete and biased information. Speaking in terms of descriptions of manufacturing companies, for both internal and external use, these characteristics seem to be the rule rather than the exception.

Concern about the long-term effects of the industrialised society, and criticism of the social forms being created by advanced industrial countries, has increased noticeably during the 1960s. These murmurings are not merely the expressions of fashionable left-wing political movements, which in fact are gradually fading, but of a feeling that mankind has never before been subjected to pressure from so many sources; that a trend which has been obvious for a long time, but hitherto has been tolerable, has moved into an era of acceleration and vast power. It seems that a qualitatively different course has recently been embarked upon, and this raises the question of why the trend started and then accelerated in an undesirable and costly direction. This book seeks to find the answer; this chapter and the preceding one have tried to indicate and explain the forces governing the form taken by technological progress, which shapes our society as a whole.

Competition, in the conventional sense, does exist and influence development, but its force is not so great as the vertical pressure militating for change which is gradually built up from basic research, applied research, and technological progress in virtually every area upon which a company depends. The situation is compulsive: there is only one possibility – to keep abreast of developments, to expand, to develop new and profitable products and technologies which will eventually lead to further expansion, and so on. While public need and the market do sometimes influence industry's decisions, they are far from being the only factors. Because of the pressure of competition and the power of the possible under which they exist, those with direct responsibility for the industrialised society have no real chance of ensuring that their choice of products is meaningful and primarily aimed at the existing unsolved problems.

The industrialised society maintains itself by its methods of measuring, evaluating, describing and managing companies. These methods are not only imperfect, based on obsolete information, and one-sided, but, most importantly, they completely ignore costs and other repercussions outside their own immediate sphere.

Developments are being brought about by forces which we obviously find it difficult to control or even explain. These forces are hidden, partly because of the fragmented economic system and partly because of imperfect measurement techniques. In short, the consequence is an alarming, unique and unprecedented situation.

Chapter 5
Our unique present-day situation

The world is heading towards macroscopic disorders – eco-logical, political and social. These threats hang over our traditional, national, ideological, and racial divisions and impose new forms of cross-boundary solidarity.

Aurelio Peccei

The second half of the twentieth century finds the human race in a historically unique situation. Never before has its position been more exposed. Never before has man faced such a threat, wherever he lives and works, whatever the colour of his skin, the nation or the class to which he belongs, whatever his political ideology or beliefs.

For the first time we are facing a global problem demanding a global solution. Our common supply of necessities, such as minerals, energy and fresh water, is being used up. Of far greater importance, however, is the fact that there is less time available than on other occasions when we have been faced with a crisis; that we can no longer escape, either literally or figuratively, to something we believe or know to be better; that in a situation of pressure where people most need to be confident of their real personal identity, this is the very thing most difficult to achieve. Of course we are aware of the gravity of the situation, but only in a fragmentary fashion, resulting partly from our own experience, partly from intuition.

In one respect we are particularly well prepared. For years alarmist reports on the danger of the earth's resources becoming exhausted have increased in volume. Figures indicate that during the last thirty years the world has consumed as much metal as man produced and consumed throughout his entire history prior to that period. We have been told that while coal mines have existed for at least 800 years, half the total coal mined has been burned during the past thirty years. Similarly, half the oil ever brought to the surface has been used during the last twelve years.

Not everything points the same way, and there are those who would disagree with this picture. Nevertheless, all serious observers are agreed that the world's resources will be exhausted within a few centuries if we continue using them at the present rate. The only debatable question is *when* this will happen; or, more precisely, how long a respite can be obtained with the aid of technology.

The civilisation of the advanced industrialised society is based on access to energy and, more important still, this energy must be easily obtainable and therefore cheap. Since the resources Nature placed at our disposal are virtually exhausted, the task facing us is to *create*, with the help of technology, fresh energy sources of a completely new kind. The probability of success in such a venture must be judged on the basis of a realisation that the entire technological culture of the West has been possible because we have lived in a world of unlimited availability of fuel. This is fast becoming a world in which most fuels are known to be in short supply.

The situation appears to be as follows. The supply of fossil fuels such as coal, oil, natural gas, etc. is so limited that we presumably only have 200–300 years in which to live on 1970 levels of consumption. If, in addition, the emerging countries were to start using the same amount of energy *per capita* as the developed countries, our stocks of fossil coal would at best last for a hundred years. Additional energy from hydro-electric schemes, use of wind-driven generators and the burning of wood can be disregarded for the sake of simplicity, since their contribution to an advanced technological civilisation can at best be marginal.

The atomic power stations, now coming into use or being projected, are based on uranium fission of such low efficiency that our supplies of uranium will only last for between 100 and 200 years at the 1970 rate of consumption. Witnessing the current growth in the number of atomic power stations based on light water reactors, it is to be expected that uranium supplies will be exhausted within a matter of decades.

It is possible that the 1980s might see the introduction of fast breeder reactors capable of using uranium much more efficiently. In this case, stocks available should be greatly increased, as it will become economically possible to exploit low-yield uranium and torium ores, but the fast breeder reactor will face us with the so-far unsolved and perhaps insoluble problem of safety. It may be that fast breeder reactors with an acceptable safety level can be built, or that scientists will be able to take the next step and build fusion reactors for which there are virtully inexhaustible supplies of fuel; the problem of safety would then be less great and the problem of radioactive waste almost negligible.

If we go further and take into account the facts concerning our total supplies of, for instance, fresh water, clean air, and necessary metals, the same pattern would emerge, and there would be general agreement that stocks will not last indefinitely. It is widely believed that solutions which are technically within our reach would push all cause for anxiety so far into the future that there would no longer be any reason to talk in terms of a brief respite. Indeed, there are some who maintain that we can come to a solution which will remove the problem once and for all. Their reasoning is usually as follows: ever since serious discussion concerning the effects of industrialisation on society began, at the end of the nineteenth century, there have been prophets of doom who forecast that this or that raw material would only last

for a few decades. However, each time the price mechanism
has operated with higher prices always leading to more
prospecting and the discovery of new profitable deposits, to
intensified re-cycling and the use of substitutes. In addition,
new technologies have been developed which have reduced
or radically altered the demands. It is maintained that there
is no reason to believe that the same pattern will not
re-emerge.

Various objections can be raised against the supposedly
positive qualities of price mechanisms. We do not create
natural resources by raising prices: we merely dig deeper
and use other deposits, pushing the problem either further
into the future or into other areas. An increase in the price
of copper, resulting from the exhaustion of deposits, might
persuade cable manufacturers and other major users of
copper to base their products on alternative metals such as
aluminium, but this, too, is only available in limited quantities, and at some time in the future is also bound to
become scarce.

With the help of the price system, we might draw heavily
in the future on one field after another, but is this not
escapism, adopting a solution which has not been thought
through to its logical conclusion? It is clear that, in practice,
the price mechanism works in such a way as to hide the
problems causing concern without solving them. As a cor-
rective, the price system's major fault is that it works too
slowly, and does not indicate from the start that certain
consequences might be undesirable; it only begins to function when the problems are just around the corner or
already looming over us.

There seems to be some sort of superstitious belief in the
ability of the market economy to adapt quickly to changed
price relationships, and it is implicitly assumed that if
the price of some scarce commodity rises, then a smaller
quantity will automatically be used. Should the price of oil
double in 1973, however, it cannot be assumed that our oil
reserves will diminish at a lower rate. On the contrary, it is

likely that the speed with which oil is used will increase for a period, and that considerable time will elapse before the total annual consumption becomes lower than it was when the higher prices were first introduced. This can, in its turn, be explained by the sluggishness which is one of the most striking characteristics of advanced industrial society.

Liberal economists sometimes speak as though they fail to realise that, because of its own impotence, the price mechanism in most countries is being replaced with a high level of industrial development. For instance, the fundamental reason for more and more direct intervention in the market economy of every Western European country is that prices are no longer an accurate reflection of the availability of resources and their exploitation. The environment becomes damaged if certain costs are not taken into account, or if they are seriously underestimated in the calculations. Certain regions suffer depopulation, since it is more profitable, from the business economy viewpoint, to concentrate production.

It is important to realise the unacceptability of a line of argument based on the conviction that the price system always ensures that resources are available. Furthermore, it is absolutely essential to understand that this point of view is basically a decision to solve the problems confronting us with the usual old remedies: it functions to defend and maintain the same pattern of development that has existed for so long.

However, on the basis of the situation existing today, it is essential to question the idea that the industrialised society should be able to solve its resources and energy problems *in the usual way*, and at the same time attend to all the other world problems. Is this hope not an extension and an expression of our traditional tendency to think in fragments? We can probably manage *one* problem, but can we manage several problems all at once?

The demands made by each separate, partial problem on science and technology are considerable; taken together, they probably cannot all be met in the time at our disposal. The development of a fusion reactor demands enormous capital investment; likewise almost any attempt to find technological solutions to the problems of reducing the future use of resources and replacing what has already been taken out would be equally costly. Capital will not be available without sacrifices. If, by means of a theoretically possible (though in practice, probably impossible) effort we could mobilise all the resources needed in these fields, what would the consequences be for the other areas on which this new technology would be founded? Repercussions on the social environment, while possibly tolerable for one project, could scarcely be so for all. It is worth speculating whether the technical and financial resources which are now earmarked for space-travel, or potential destruction, would be sufficient for the task; but can we believe that the national, political and economic divisions between individuals and groups of people could be ironed out so quickly that the enterprise could be undertaken communally? How likely is it that the stupidity, intolerance and sluggishness which are so characteristic of this age could speedily be transformed into the required breadth of vision, view of the whole perspective, and tolerant approach?

However, even if the necessary technology, resources, and social and political preconditions could really be met, would we be in a better position? In practice, might it not mean that we would flock to those who maintain that, with the help of technology, we can be sure that "... the earth's resources will last for a long time yet"?[6] However, this is fundamentally a cynical and self-sufficient attitude. The question is not whether it will take 100, 200 or 2,000 years before all resources are exhausted; the fact is, that sooner or later, and in the long-term perspective *very soon*, we shall have reached that point. How far into the future does Tor Ragnar Gerholm's responsibility for coming generations stretch? Does it stop with his children, his grandchildren, or his great grand-children?

There are those who believe that we can overcome our difficulties, that with the help of technology we can, as before, save ourselves from the limitations imposed on us by reduced supplies, and achieve something like a land flowing with milk and honey (a stage which the American futurologist, Herman Kahn, has rather more prosaically called the "post-industrial era". Some doubt this, but all are agreed that this is probably the first time that man not only believes his resources are becoming exhausted: he *knows* it.

However, reduced stocks of fossil coal, uranium, and necessary metals are only part of this sombre and historically unique picture. Never before has mankind had so little time in which to put things to rights, yet the realisation that time is running out is extremely important. Otherwise it can easily be argued that man has perpetually faced difficulties, but has always discovered techniques for surmounting them. However, there is now a fundamental difference – when man has previously been faced with a serious situation which has influenced him and removed the foundations on which his customary way of life is based, he has almost without exception had hundreds, perhaps even thousands, of years in which to adapt to the changed circumstances. Moreover, the crisis conditions have tended to be local or regional, but rarely have reached global proportions.

We now stand at a crossroads which, in some ways, resembles that which our ancestors faced when forced to abandon their life in the treetops. While those driven down from the trees had millions of years in which to adapt to new and dangerous surroundings, today's rapidly accelerating technological development has "thrown us into a situation in which we must make an extremely rapid decision, and in which the choice we make must be based on thought and foresight and not dictated by chance circumstances".

The pressure of the modern age is particularly striking in relation to the question of the exhaustion of resources. Summarising, we know that during the past thirty years, the amount of metal used has equalled the total produced and consumed by mankind throughout the whole of its previous history. Assuming that consumption continues at its present rate, 80 per cent of the world's total oil supplies will be used within the next fifty to sixty years. After that some 10 per cent of the original deposits would be left, since a certain percentage has already been consumed, and we could reckon on oil supplies running out completely by 2100. However, it is much more interesting to assume that oil consumption rises annually by the same percentage as during the 1960s, and to base our assumptions on two alternative estimates of the quantity of oil available in the earth. One estimate is pessimistic, the other optimistic in assuming approximately double the quantity. The pessimistic assessment gives 1985 as the date by which demand will greatly exceed supply. However, if twice as much oil is available, the date will be 1995!

The influence of time can also be seen in an entirely different respect. The interval between a basic discovery and its commercial or practical exploitation is reduced year by year, as witness the well-known sequence: telephone, fifty-six years; radio, thirty-five years; television, twelve years. Each innovation of this kind has incalculable repercussions on the organisation and work of the human race. What happens is a type of revolution closely linked to the actual "tool" discovered, with a far greater significance than that ascribed to those events we normally refer to as revolutions. Paul Valéry, in his reflections on historical progress, points out that certain important events are not mentioned in history books. "An event taking place over more than a century is not found mentioned in any document." His remark is revealing for two reasons. Firstly, he puts the problem in the right perspective, and thereby shows himself to be a fore-runner (since he wrote this at least forty years ago) of ways of thought which have subsequently appeared original and exciting to many others. Secondly, his comment points to and underlines the tremendous periods of time which, in an earlier age, characterised the innovation process. Things are different now: the very speed with which we introduce new and comprehensive technologies masks a hidden resistance which is probably historically unique. History certainly alludes to many violent protests against new methods and equipment. The medieval guilds resisted "technological changes" (so far as these actually took place at that time) because the guild members feared that new methods of production would undermine the security and safety which their privileged position ensured them. The council of the city of Danzig, fearing unemployment on account of a band loom invented in the seventeenth century, had the inventor secretly strangled. However, there were two essential differences: either the changes did not even affect the entire population of a country, let alone the entire population of the world, or else they were introduced over a period lasting for a generation or more, often over centuries. For instance, our surprise today at the abilities of the computer is largely determined by the fact that we have had only ten – or at the most twenty – years in which to meet its challenge and almost unlimited capacity. The healthy respect for, and opposition to, innovations is reinforced according to the degree and intensity of the change concerned. For example, if the technical solution to the energy problem, sketched above, were to be initiated, the demand for change would probably be on a hitherto unknown scale. Even if historians could establish that tolerance towards technological innovations has gradually increased since before the Industrial Revolution, the process still could not be carried out without serious disturbances. This is the second dimension of the influence of time.

The pressure exerted by the dwindling supplies of what we consider necessities, coupled with the influence of the related pressure of time, are two aspects of the changed conditions which make the present position unique. The third component is a realisation of the close interrelationship between all things and, perhaps particularly, the resultant limitation of freedom of action. It may well be that this is the most serious and important of the partial aspects. Until some time ago society was fragmented and atomistic but, to continue along this parallel, it can be argued that after 1830 the social structure in England took on the aspect of molecules rather than single atoms. Today we are approaching something with the character of a globally interrelated structure.

Whatever aspect of human activities and their consequences is considered, whether scientific, economic or political, the same pattern of development can be found. To begin with there were islands of independence, and developments tended to have influence in one sphere only. Then came a limited degree of interaction. Now we have comprehensive interdependence, offering little opportunity for autonomy. A historian has filled thirteen pages with a list of important inventions and scientific discoveries, mainly from the nineteenth century, which were made by two or more people independently of each other at more or less the same time. This could scarcely happen today. With virtually a free interchange of fundamental scientific information from one country to another, and with sophisticated retrieval systems, knowledge will soon become internationalised in a very real sense.

The trend is more or less identical in any field of development, since all the characteristics of the industrialised society – prices, market, finance, technology, management methods etc. – are, to a constantly increasing extent, tied in with each other and, furthermore, work together with a significant degree of harmony. All the repercussions such as monetary crises, destruction of the environment, alienation and so on, are by their very nature global and general in a way hitherto unknown.

In one significant respect, however, it seems that this irresistible drive towards internationalisation, interdependence, and a lack of autonomy has been successfully halted; or at least it has not asserted itself to anything approaching the extent experienced elsewhere. Apart from marginal changes, independent nations have maintained their shapes over several centuries; while they have become more sensitive to international events, powerful forces which see it as their prime objective to defend national independence have been very successful in their efforts to stand firm in the face of pressure to integrate. This is an anachronistic state of affairs which in the long run could have the most serious consequences.

This understanding of the way in which everything is interrelated makes it easier to follow Marcus Wallenberg when he maintains that the assertion that individual company managements have room for manoeuvre in any given situation is a vast exaggeration. Changes occur far more as a result of the preconditions for the firm's activities than through management decisions to introduce specific measures. It also becomes easier to understand why, in a capitalist economy predominantly run by private capital, state enterprises are never able to function according to their own ideas or in conditions which vary from those in the world around.

We can no longer retreat. We can only temporarily escape from environmental destruction and excessive social pressure. We cannot avoid oil pollution far out to sea, or sulphur dioxide in the mountain air. We can no longer find solitude – even in the most inaccessible places. Furthermore, we can find no religion, no economic system or political ideology which can claim to have the answer to our dilemma. If this diagnosis is correct, we are in a unique situation.

The predicament is partly a result of our relationship to Nature. Rolf Edberg, who appears more capable than most people of elucidating and pinpointing the seriousness of the situation, believes that our close relationship with our natural surroundings is about to undergo a change for the worse. Primitive man lived not only *in* Nature, but *with* it. The sense of rootlessness produced by the increasing distance between civilisation and Nature has been bad enough, but the fact that we can no longer approach the Nature which enchants us without a feeling of suspicion, has desperately alarming prospects which have not yet been appreciated.

Exhausted reserves, the pressure of time, and a closely woven pattern of interdependence can, perhaps, provide not only the basis for profound changes, but also sufficient evidence to demonstrate that the situation is unique in itself. But the real pressure to create new forms and to think in new ways will probably come from within ourselves, and it is here that the realisation that mankind will no longer accept or even tolerate the general pattern of development is probably highly significant.

The pressure on mankind is not only tremendous, but peculiar to the age; it seems that traditional viewpoints and well established situations have been completely transformed. At one time we were subjected to physical pressures: nowadays there are psychological. At one time industrial work was primarily physically exhausting, but now, due to the increasing tempo, it is first and foremost psychologically wearing. Previously, the long working day and the need to work in order to survive were the burdens, while in the modern advanced industrialised society there is the psychological fear of unemployment. This last point is worth pursuing.

It is highly likely that, in view of the manner in which advanced industrial society functions and the divisions between nations and their different economic systems, it will be impossible to maintain full employment. No policies which have so far been devised to deal with the labour market will be able to prevent the trend towards unemployment; on the contrary, it is very possible that we shall soon be forced to consider whether the policies so far adopted on the labour market are the right ones. Sven Fagerberg says that the sacred doctrine of full employment justifies everything; everything can be committed in its name, no folly is too great, no river too wide, no interference too high-handed.

The Sweden of today cannot be considered a society of full employment. Indeed, only about half the adult population is fully employed and there are potentially something like a hundred thousand people seeking work. It is important to realise that the tendency to under-employment and unemployment is only marginally connected with the economic policy of the country, but is more a consequence of the industrial society's choice of technology on the one hand and its shrinking resources and markets on the other. Herman Kahn, admittedly, says that talk of unemployment in what he calls "the post-industrial society at its zenith" is a misleading description of the real situation. In an imaginary situation where there was an abundance of financial and other resources, or when cold or actively aggressive wars, or communications with distant planets resulted in constantly unsatiated markets, then the suggestion might be right – temporarily.

However, the explanation is simple enough. If, on the one hand, productivity constantly increases, and if a certain number of people continue to produce more goods and services each year than in the preceding year, then there is naturally only one way in which each person can keep his job – by creating a need for more goods and services. If, on the other hand, there is a shortage of resources, or if the market becomes saturated, it is just as certain that fewer jobs will be available. This is a simple way of expressing the problem which faces the advanced industrialised society today. On account of the structure of the economic system, the movement towards an ever more efficient technology is irresistible (an assertion which was partly explained in the last chapter and which will be further discussed in the next). In order to satisfy the capacity of new technology with new markets able to absorb the ever-increasing supply of goods and services, it will be necessary either to resort to methods which might appear artificial and, perhaps, of dubious ethical value, or to exploit scarce and expensive resources. It is in this context that Sven Fagerberg's remark concerning the sacred doctrine of full employment must be seen. The desperate search for new products and markets, and the importance of economic wear, can be recognised as signs that we have entered a new era where the inevitable movement towards fewer jobs can only be hidden by the greatest exertions and the most suspect methods. The counterargument – that experience shows increased productivity to have led, via wage fixing, to increased production and thereby to more jobs – has no value at all unless accompanied by the admission that this process depends on more resources being found to meet the increased demand and on the creation of an unsatisfied need for more goods in those who earn larger disposable incomes. Contrary to common belief, technology is not neutral in this respect; it has many different guises. Technological development does not, in all its forms, lead to unemployment: the responsibility lies only with such innovations as inevitably seem to create, not merely a constant stream of even more productive technology, but also one which continues to erode scarce resources and to stretch the environment to its limit.

The links between increased productivity, higher wages and fresh jobs have been taken for granted to such an extent, especially during the past few decades, that many people have difficulty in realising how things have changed. Our planet is not so big after all. Far from being infinite, its resources are steadily diminishing – despite the fact that, at most, only a third of the world's population enjoys a reasonable standard of living (calculated no higher than any income above subsistence level). This kind of information gives ample cause for reflection, but it is also worth noting that people living in advanced industrialised countries are increasingly unwilling to "consume" the type of technology being developed. One thing is certain: if technology continues to expand at its present rate it will be impossible to maintain full employment.

What has so far been understood by the concept of "work" can, of course, be changed. It should be possible to define "full employment" as one day's work per week, the rest of the time being divided between leisure and study, though this is obviously a privilege limited to developed countries. However, the decisive factor is not this kind of hair-splitting, but whether or not people could adapt to that type of life-style. There is, in fact, no really convincing reason why we should prefer not to work rather than to work; indeed it can be argued that work, more than anything else, creates a background of security against which existence can be experienced. Changes in man's biological status occur very slowly: it probably takes hundreds of thousands of years for any fundamental steps to be achieved. Taking an evolutionary perspective, man has always had to struggle for his very existence; therefore if, within a matter of centuries, he is not only to be given a materially better and more secure life, but also to be freed from work, this development is unlikely to take place without repercussions which would place humanity in a situation of stress. The striving to achieve improved material standards, social welfare and security, coupled with the belief that what is lacking is even better material standards, even better social welfare and even greater security might well, in time, turn out to be mistakes.

One expression of a widespread dissatisfaction with conditions so far, is the fact that the demands now making themselves felt for better communication, increased influence, and independence of action at work, are not local or regional phenomena but – to varying degrees – affect the whole of the industrialised world. The owner's right to decide is being questioned more and more widely, and in an increasing number of work environments. It may well be that these forces simply reflect the feeling that a company or organisation ought not merely to be a place where people work, but where they *live* – in the true sense of the word. However, it is more likely that what has produced this trend is both the twofold pressure from increasing demands for further rationalisation and change and the feeling of impotence resulting from the impersonality, difficulty of access

and sheer physical distance from the people making
decisions and the places where decisions are made. If the
cost of staff in a company rises by ten per cent annually,
while the number of employees remains the same, this
produces an incredible pressure to increase productivity and
to expand. As has been argued, expansion can be said to be
the principal way in which firms seek to reduce the pressure
of costs. However, the increase in volume has only partly
lessened the need to rationalise and to develop new and
more efficient production technologies. This in its turn
increases pressure on those working in the firm, and the
unions find themselves in a kind of vicious circle because – if
they are to maintain the economic balance of society – to be
able to offer workers higher wages presupposes rationalisation and labour-saving equipment which, in turn, lead to a
reduction in the work force, and so on. This is one side of
the question.

Until quite recently a company could almost always be
identified with its owner. When he studied the large firms of
his day, Karl Marx was able to link the new wealth and the
miserable working conditions to individuals or to single
families. All the power and the right to make decisions were
concentrated in one person, to whom dislike, fury, responsibility or approval could be directed. Today power has
moved deeper and deeper into the organisation; decisions
are increasingly reached through group work and are based
on statistical evidence. The outsider has no real opportunity
to discover where responsibility lies or where to direct his
criticisms. This is the other side of the picture and, taken
together, these two factors result in an increasing demand
for some form of workers' participation in the company's
activities.

The incipient opposition to innovations must also be seen
in this context. If the director of a large manufacturing
company were asked which factors could be said to militate
most against a radical technological or administrative reorganisation of the company, he would probably reply that

opposition would come from within the organisation itself. He would hardly be likely to lay the blame on either the unions or the country's financial policies as the principal causes. Any major innovation not only dislocates the firm's activities, but also creates social and psychological pressures.

There is another side to people's increasing distaste for the new situation. Irrespective of whether the growth society uses up its resources, or whether the time left to solve its problems is shorter than ever before, life becomes less rich and more disturbed when things are merely glossed over.

Statistically speaking the result of an economic process, on the lines of and according to the conditions dictated by the capitalist system, is that, over a lengthy time, production grows by a certain average percentage each year; in other words, it has the character of what in mathematical language is termed "exponential growth". The exponential growth function has a quality all of its own – at first nothing happens, and the interval required to double the unit being studied, for instance, is very long. Subsequent intervals, however, become progressively shorter, which means that the graph, plotting the growth, will end by pointing straight upwards.

Taking as examples the world's population or total industrial production, to say that they have grown exponentially over the centuries is only modified truth. At most it can be said that if, with the aid of a few points of reference, we were to make a diagram of how population and industry have grown, the result would look like a graph of the exponential function. If more points of reference were available, it would be possible to discover that the developments have, at least in the case of economic growth, been irregular and characterised by periodic leaps. Historians believe that the course of progress can be described as relatively brief and presumably painful periods of change alternating with periods of stability, rather than the "permanent" steady progress implied by exponential growth. The only thing we know for certain is that world population and industrial production are now both growing exponentially. This state of affairs cannot possibly continue.

However, population and industrial production are not the only things to be growing exponentially. The use of natural resources, gross national products, the number of airline passengers, road accidents, and university examinations – all these grow in the same way. So, too, does the amount of information available (which is not the same as the value of that information) and, perhaps most thought-provoking of all, the extent of our knowledge. Possibly this is what Glenn Seaborg has in mind when he speaks of the coming decades as a race between the information society and the forces of destruction.

Irrespective of whether it be world population, our own knowledge or Volvo's turnover, it is obvious, if measured correctly, that growth cannot continue indefinitely in this way. This is purely and simply natural law. If population growth cannot be contained by means of family planning and other measures, the trend is bound to be towards uncontrollable – and in the long run, catastrophic – growth, says Tor Ragnar Gerholm. "The population of the world will realise this sooner or later." But what incredible human suffering lies hidden in this prospect. Even if, within a few decades, and with the help of medical techniques, persuasion, force or understanding on the part of those affected, the population explosion could be halted, the population pyramid would still be shaped in such a way that the majority would continue to be supported by the minority – with all that this implies in the way of frustration and the distribution of resources.

Many biological processes seem to show a kind of natural wisdom; for example, when accelerating growth reaches a certain stage, it is often followed by a fall in numbers so that, overall, growth levels out and is maintained at a suitable rate. This is true of the formation of certain antibodies, as when blood plasma replaces lost blood and tissue cells in the case of injury. Sooner or later anything with an exponential pattern of growth must pass through this stage, the only phenomenon which can expect a permanent natural moratorium being one able to show that its growth takes place without reliance on insufficient resources.

Until quite recently, man has had not only abundant resources but time at his disposal in which to adapt to change; until now he has always had a chance to find a better place somewhere or other, rather than remaining in one unsuitable to his needs; until recent years he has, by and large, felt himself to be firmly rooted in existence. All this merely indicates that man is under the influence of the forces at play in the final stages of an exponential growth pattern that is on the verge of an asymptote (a line which continually approaches a given curve, but does not meet it within a finite distance).

Chapter 6
A balanced economic system

In an open system permanence in itself can be an indication that forces are at work.

Walter Cannon

You cannot enter the same river twice.

Cratylus

The acceleration of growth will be stopped. This might be brought about by strong, determined actions on the part of far-sighted politicians, businessmen or even ordinary people. Or it might happen of its own accord, though in this case the process will undoubtedly be more painful, frustrating and costly.

A decisive question is, naturally, what chances has the Western economic system, the "mixed economy" as it is known, of bringing about a stable, balanced state of affairs without making profound changes in its method of functioning? This question has two dimensions: is the capitalist industrial system capable of a *quantitative* change into a non-expanding position? And can it *qualitatively* adapt to the demands of the world around for a meaningful contribution; demands which will doubtless be expressed more strongly and articulately in a failing economy?

First let us deal with the quantitative aspect. Can a modern capitalist economy function at all without growth? Can a modern Swedish or American company survive without an annual increase in turnover? The questions need not necessarily lead to the same conclusion, but they are closely connected, and a simple analogy might indicate the answer.

Any economic system which needs to grow, or even to maintain the *status quo*, must make a profit; in this respect Nature gives no special privileges to feudal, capitalist, socialist, or communist social systems. In an economically static society, such as the feudal system, the surplus had to be sufficiently large at least to keep the serfs in a reasonable condition, replace worn-out tools and machines, replenish empty barns and stores, etc. The idea of surplus was thus a reality.

If we talk of profit in monetary terms, however, it is important to remember that money is only a symbol of surplus. This is perhaps central to the understanding of an economic system. On the one hand there is a tangible production force of people, machines and technical knowledge, and on the other there is a symbol of the real situation, which we usually call the economic system. It is difficult to distinguish between reality and symbol, since the symbol has taken on such importance that it has acquired its own concrete and tangible forms of expression – money, banks, cash dispensers and professors of economics.

The distinction between the symbol and reality is, however, essential if we are to obtain an answer to the question as to whether a capitalist economy *has* to expand. Careful consideration shows that reality makes no such demand; not, at least, to an extent which would explain the growth we see around us. At some time in the past when such a hypothesis as this had some basis in reality, human curiosity, greed and desire for change, together with encouragement and orders from further up in the hierarchy, might have contributed to what we now call an increase in productivity. But on the whole the driving force behind progress must be sought in the construction of the image, or rather in its ability to strengthen mankind's tendency to look for progress. It may seem a commonplace, but it is important to point out that the image has gradually transformed reality, and that reality in its turn has transformed the image.

Thus the first step is clear – the answer must be found in the economic system. How did it happen that we were forced to create a world of symbols alongside the world of reality? A simple answer would be to say that it was because of the way in which we have found it convenient to arrange our social activities, or, in more concrete terms, it turned out to be practical for the strong man to fight, the intelligent man to think, the man living by the sea to fish. This resulted in the evolution of a system in which this fragmented reality could be turned into a unity. We were forced to create some token, which subsequently evolved into money, as a symbol for something else. It is painfully obvious, but important to appreciate, that at that "moment" (a moment extending over hundreds of years) we took the step from reality to a world of symbols.

The consequences were incalculable. With the help of his symbols man could extend his right of ownership far beyond the parameters which had hitherto been in force. This realisation places the right of ownership in its correct perspective. To be a multi-millionaire, to own vast and distant factories or estates, is an absurdity in reality but possible in the world of symbols. If we imagined (and we can only imagine, since progress has made such a situation impossible in reality) that a Howard Hughes, an Aristotle Onassis, or a Marcus Wallenberg lived in the world as it was prior to the invention of the symbol, they would have been confronted by an impossible choice – either, figuratively speaking, to drown in their own assets, or be forced to exist in several places simultaneously.

The message of this abstract and unwieldy metaphor is that the very introduction of symbols in place of reality made it possible to accumulate, and thereby to acquire, the right of decision over assets without actually having them in one's possession. This is the really dynamic element in the economic system.

Now the question will arise as to how man gradually developed an almost pathological lust for symbols, that is, for the material representations of wealth. Anthropologists appear to agree that it is necessary to distinguish between Western civilisation and other cultures. An economic interpretation of the cultural pattern seems to be more valid for our own civilisation than for others with which we are acquainted. The ambition to acquire possessions in the peculiar way adopted by Western civilisation in order to give expression to its own personality is also true of socialist systems following the Soviet pattern. A touch of greed, a little envy and a large proportion of Protestant ethics have probably all contributed to accelerating the process of accumulation. Individuals, groups of people, businesses and nations have all been influenced by it.

However, this is only a partial explanation. To these contributory factors must be added those created by the economic systems themselves. In a primitive society it is difficult to envisage a concept such as bankruptcy having any real meaning. The harvest might fail or the fishing might be poor, people would suffer and material and immaterial values would be affected; but these are rules created by Nature itself – by reality. Bankruptcy is an expression of the rules made up by our world of symbols.

Interplay between reality and the symbol gradually widened the distance between the individual's contribution and the final product. Not only was reality fashioned by more and more bricks, but each tiny unit was split into still smaller fractions. In addition to explaining why some means of exchange became necessary, this metaphor expresses in concrete terms the necessity for a symbol able to reflect the limitations by which reality is characterised. Or, in other words, if an individual or a firm cannot pay for the goods and services received and used in various activities, then this economic unit is subjected to sanctions by way of being declared bankrupt.

A small but important link in this chain of cause and effect is still missing. There are a large number of economic units of varying sizes – individuals, families, organisations, business firms, nations and so on. At a specific time all these units have certain assets, and the only way to maintain these is by creating a surplus. Since both assets and surpluses can be translated into monetary terms, it is possible to separate the right of control from the concept of physical possession, this process being reinforced by a host of formal and informal rules and regulations governing financial behaviour. Specialisation, which leads to further interdependence, produces still more rules in the sense that the prize – the symbol of surplus in the capitalist system – must be sufficiently large to guarantee survival, and this means more than merely keeping a financial position intact.

However, since profit in a developed economic system is the difference between what others pay for my services and what I myself have to pay for occasional or permanent help in order to supply these services, it is clear that any change in the economic systems with which our own is interrelated must produce significant repercussions. An endeavour to expand markets, raise prices or reduce costs becomes a way of life, in fact a necessity. It becomes important to make constant use of profit (which, to a certain extent, we are entitled to do in the capitalist system) in order to expand and improve the firm, simply because our competitors are doing the same. This is the missing link in the chain of cause and effect.

The answer to the question posed at the beginning of this chapter, as to whether a capitalist system, of its own accord, is capable of reducing the rate of expansion and reaching a state of balance, must therefore be in the negative. This is not, as many believe, because capitalism is based on a monetary economic system in which profit is an important concept. Nor is it, as is even more widely believed, because

the means of production are in private hands. Instead, the
fundamental reason is to be found in the interplay between
the individual's right to do as he likes with *his* net profit, and
the equal right of others, who influence but cannot be
influenced, to do as they like with *their* net profits. It is the
structure of the system which is to blame.

The limitations of the theory of surplus value

A more detailed discussion of these ideas might be appropriate at this stage, since the simplified scheme of things
developed above provides an opportunity to discuss one of
the central features of Marxist thought – the theory of
surplus value.

Karl Marx and his followers define the idea of surplus
value in the following manner: if the productivity of work
carried out is so low that the earnings from the labour of one
individual are not sufficient to do more than simply supply
his own needs, then there is no social benefit from his work.
All are producers and are in the same state of poverty. But
every increase in productivity, over and above this minimum
level, creates the possibility of some surplus, and, in the
words of Ernest Mandel: ". . . as soon as two hands create
more than is necessary for their own needs the basis is
created for disagreement on the way in which this surplus
should be distributed."

From this hypothetical moment work is divided into two
categories – the amount which is required to maintain the
producer, and the remainder. It can also be formulated in
another way by saying that as the producer carries out the
necessary work he also achieves the necessary production,
and in achieving a work surplus he also produces a social
surplus. Surplus value is no more than an expression, in
economic terms, of the social surplus.

However, more traditional book-keeping terminology will
say that surplus value is the gross profit minus all expenses,

or, expressed differently, the net profit plus taxes, sales, payments and interest. The Marxist will argue that the net income cannot be a reasonable and realistic measure of the surplus. The following quotation, with its practical approach, might be said to reflect the modern Marxist's view of surplus value:

> "Stora Kopparbergs Bergslags Ltd., which is one of the major shareholders in the Grängesberg Company, is a combination of forestry, timber and paper companies as well as mining and steel firms. . . . Total wages, including salaries to executives, management and directors were 323 million kronor in 1968, while sales amounted to 1,303 millions. The company possesses its own power station, so that in that particular year there was almost a thousand million kronor to account for surplus value, oil, minor purchases of raw materials and the wear and tear on machinery over and above what the firm's own workers were able to undertake in the firm's own workshops. In 1968, then, the total surplus value was . . . nearer a thousand million kronor, or three to four times as much as the 236 millions distributed in wages and salaries to all their workers."[7]

If we ignore taxes, then the essence of the Marxist calculation of profit, in other words his calculation of surplus value, is that the replacement of capital cannot be considered as costs. Here it must be borne in mind that "capital" is taken to mean interest on borrowed capital and payment of dividends, the latter also being regarded as capital borrowing.

This must be a false view, founded on a mixture of the constructed model of reality (the economic system) and reality itself. Financial capital is nothing but a symbol of reality, for if someone invests a million kronor in a company it is not only a sheet of paper, but indirectly represents goods and services. What we can criticise and deprecate is the fact that we have built up a society in which the organisation of work necessitates the construction of a model of that society which, in its turn, makes it possible for assets to be accumulated and for the right to take decisions to be concentrated in a few hands. However, this does not imply that the replacement of capital as such is wrong or that it should be overlooked. The cost of capital cannot be ignored either in a capitalist economy, or – and this point is not widely realised – in an advanced economic system based on the distribution of work and an open market. Should an attempt be made to do so, the main result would be a less effective allocation of scarce resources and planning difficulties; in other words "a spanner in the works".

The theory of surplus value is undoubtedly a politically effective instrument, almost a work of genius, and it can be readily understood how Marx, as a politician, realised its potential. On the other hand it is doubtful whether, as a brilliant intellectual, he was serious in his insistence that "the ruling class" is accumulating surplus value for its own benefit. He must have realised quite clearly that although the capitalist system certainly created inequalities of income it was, historically speaking, principally a redistribution among established classes, from the feudal lord through the merchant capitalist to the factory owner. More important, however, was the fact that, throughout all this period from about 1200 to 1850, a gradual change in income ratios had taken place between the privileged and the under-privileged. It has been estimated that in the agrarian societies the established classes, which constituted 1–2 per cent of the population, received at least 50 per cent of the total incomes, a ratio which had noticeably grown even by the middle of the nineteenth century. On the question of whether the increasing equality also included a redistribution of power and privilege, Gerhard Lenski is among those who have argued that the emergence of the industrialised society marked a significant shift towards greater equality in comparison with former years. Marx must have been aware of these facts.

Moreover, Marx must have known that, even if very large incomes were at the disposal of the capitalist, they were not squandered largely on a life of luxury, as had been the case under the feudal system, but were reinvested. Indeed, this can be said to be the hallmark of capitalism. In this respect Jacob Fugger ("the Rich", 1459–1525) personified the capitalist spirit. He considered wealth to be the basis upon which to gather greater wealth, hence on the grounds of his fundamental principles, the amount he retained for his own consumption was kept to a minimum.

Old and new stagnation theories

For centuries, economists and political thinkers have discussed and formulated various "stagnation theories". Ideas of this nature have been clearly related to the state of the market, in the sense that having become the focus of attention and undergone development in times of economic failure, they have then slowly been submerged with the return of better times. Certain stagnation theories were formulated in Sweden during a crisis which occurred towards the end of the nineteenth century, but it was notably during the 1930s that they made their mark. It was argued that the gap between potential and actual production should be widened, as should that between potential and actual employment. Unemployment was expected to increase gradually. Economic growth was to be reduced, and possibly even transformed into economic decline. There were considered to be three main reasons why stagnation was thought to be unavoidable:

(1) Markets were on the point of becoming saturated and disappearing; those propounding this view could see no signs of new frontiers.

(2) Technology had already reached and passed its zenith, and the most profitable technological steps had already been taken. Either the marginal profitability of new technology

could be expected to be so low that it would never be developed, or else – and this was a slightly more subtle argument – it was felt that the only technology left to invest in would demand vast amounts of capital.

(3) A fall in the population growth in the capitalist world could be expected to inhibit the economy.

Since then, Joseph Schumpeter has successfully refuted all these and other arguments along similar lines. The fact that no new geographical frontiers are to be found is not the same as saying that there are no further opportunities for economic expansion. He suggests that, from the viewpoint of explaining and supporting growth, the conquest of the air might well turn out to be as important as was the conquest of India in its day. As for the marginal use of new technology, he makes the obvious comment that the development of a new technology, as opposed to the cultivation of a hitherto unused field, will not result in lower productivity than that already in use. He entirely refutes the demographic argument.

Raymond Aron supports Schumpeter's analysis by means of slightly different but closely related arguments. His additional observation that what we have to fear is not a shrinking market but the exhaustion of natural resources is highly significant. "If there are no natural resources to support production there will obviously be an insuperable obstacle in the way of further growth." He adds, "But that time has not yet arrived", although it is doubtful whether this reservation is as valid in 1972 as it was when he made it in 1955.

There is a different, more subtle and perhaps newer stagnation theory, which argues that economic growth automatically slows down when more and more workers leave the productive occupations – such as agriculture, forestry and industry – in order to work on what have been called "tertiary" and "quartiary" occupations. The argument that the capital investment required for each worker in these jobs is much lower than, for instance, in industry, can be explained by the fact that productivity can scarcely be increased by the replacement of labour with capital: in other words, "a barber does not cut more heads of hair per day now than a hundred years ago". Hence growth must gradually slow down. When there is a minimum number of workers in primary and secondary occupations we shall have reached what some call the "stationary economy". This is an argument reminiscent of the demographic theory, and is based on the same fundamental misunderstanding – the belief that an increase in the production of goods and services will automatically be reduced with a drop in the number of workers employed on them. Moreover, to put it simply, it is doubtful whether the investment per employee in the so-called "non-productive" occupations is so very much smaller than in industry. It can probably be shown that for large and growing groups of tertiary and quartiary employment it is in fact higher.

There is a significant difference between earlier stagnation theorists and those of today. The economists who debated the question in the 1930s aimed at demonstrating either the inevitable stagnation of the capitalist economy – possibly even its total destruction at some future time – or, on the contrary, that the danger signals heralding such an event were being exaggerated. Today a Jay Forrester, Aurelio Peccei or Alexander King would maintain that all economic systems, irrespective of whether they are termed capitalist or socialist, must replace the acceleration of growth by balance and stability; in the long run this means stagnation.

The impossibility of full employment

Examination of a specific but representative industrial concern in Sweden shows not only the obvious fact that its turnover is increasing, but also that its turnover *must* increase. Today, it is almost impossible for Swedish industry to maintain its profitability without expansion. At the same time this pattern is repeated, in all important respects, in any country where the economy is based on a decentralised right to administer net profits.

If a manufacturer is asked what forces operate towards expansion, he will point to the pressure of prices on his own products, coupled with both the increased costs of labour, and the impossibility of avoiding a reduction in his gross profit as a result of rationalisation and increased production. Such a state of affairs creates the need for a constant increase in turnover. It is possible to demonstrate that the part played by wages in the increased total value of Swedish industry has progressively risen from approximately 70 per cent over the past ten years and that the gross profit has accordingly fallen. However, it would be an oversimplification to conclude from this, as has been done before, that increased wage demands are the principal factors in expansion. There is no doubt at all that pressure is exerted by wages, but it is more important to realise that the interaction between a company's own actions and those taking place outside the firm gradually builds up a pressure which influences but cannot be influenced, which threatens the manufacturer but is outside his control. It originates beyond his immediate orbit, and is exerted through customers, competitors, suppliers, authorities and so on, all of whom are in turn influenced by others, who are influenced by others yet again. Consequently, in a developed economy there is not one manufacturing company which, to any significant extent, can be said to have freedom of action when faced with the question of whether or not to expand. This realisation makes it possible to assert, for instance, that over the next few years the iron and steel industry in Sweden will be *obliged* to increase its production by 10 per cent per annum in order to survive.

From such a perspective, it is easier to understand that full employment and technological progress are incompatible and merely serve to work against each other. If technology continues to develop along the lines it has so far followed in the highly industrialised society, it will simply become impossible to provide meaningful employment for all those who can and will produce something. The assurances which politicians in more industrial countries have to give, that the introduction of strong measures will ensure full employment, become mere voices crying in the wilderness. Either they will have to tell the voters that the path we are treading will result in an increasing scarcity of jobs, or else – to the accompaniment of more re-training, defence work and measures to manipulate the labour market – they will have to give more and more frequent and categorical assurances that things will become better "next year", until eventually the situation becomes completely untenable.

In the previous chapter we attempted to sketch the background to the present situation. Companies cannot allow themselves the luxury of a pause in their expansion programmes or their efforts to increase the efficiency of their activities. Orthodox competition over prices, service, quality and, to an even greater extent, over the vertical pressure to produce still more efficient and attractive products as a result of research and development, simply does not permit manufacturers to slacken off in their efforts to improve their own products and reduce them in price. This inflexibility arises because our economic system is constructed on the basis of a series of independent units which, while they do not even possess the freedom to decide for themselves what to do with their profits (after payment of tax and interest on borrowed capital), are all under pressure to ensure that their activities *do* yield a profit. In brief, any industrial concern which did not constantly exploit every opportunity to sell more, and to make a better product at a lower cost, would quite consciously reduce its capacity to make a profit and thereby, in the long run, start on the path to inevitable economic death. If expansion cannot be achieved by way of increased sales, or if the expansion achieved by these means is insufficient, then, as an integral part of this process, people will lose their jobs. This is not a flexible rule relating only to individual firms or to certain branches of industry: it permeates and dominates our whole system of economic activities. Constant efforts to produce more and to rationalise production are typical of all capitalist societies. Through the rationalisation of structure, and conscious measures to improve the economic framework, people are moved from less productive positions to those spheres of production which offer greater possibilities for expansion and increased efficiency. It is thought-provoking and symptomatic that of the gross investments of developed countries some 60–70 per cent are devoted to rationalisation and new forms of technology for increasing efficiency, the ultimate aim of which is to replace labour by capital. Naturally, this process creates new job-opportunities, but not – and this is the important factor – at the same rate at which the old ones are disappearing. Contrary to what was foreseen by industry itself and the long-term predictions in 1955, there was no rise in the numbers employed in industry in the second half of the 1960s. This hard fact should be seen by those in authority as a sign that further expansion will become more difficult and eventually impossible. The stage will soon be reached where technological efficiency will not only have covered all the needs which industrial and market planners can conceive, but will also have quite decisively monopolised the available resources. If the capitalist system's manner of functioning today is to be continued in the future, the efficiency of the production apparatus will constantly be increased; since production itself is directed in such a way as to make expansion difficult or impossible, it will be impracticable in the long term to maintain full employment.

If we believe that the economic system must stop growing at its present rate, we must face the inevitable question as to exactly what will have to stagnate. Does stagnation mean that the sales of individual companies must not increase? Does it imply that they may increase mathematically but not geometrically? Or does it mean that investments must gradually level out? In future, must the sums spent on new investments or on reinvestment remain constant? There is probably no universally valid answer to all these questions or, if there is, it must be so vague as to be meaningless: something like "all growth must stop".

Through their experiments designed to simulate complex social systems, Jay Forrester and his colleagues have perhaps provided us with the best attempt at an informed guess. Their work with a "world model", the preliminary results of which have recently been published, indicates two essential qualities in the complex reality comprising all the activities on this planet. The model, which is greatly simplified and has indeed been criticised in this respect, indicates on the one hand that complex systems often behave in an unexpected manner and, on the other, that partial solutions are insufficient.

Even without strenuous thought, common sense tells us that the necessary change is a 25 per cent reduction in the rate at which natural resources are being exploited; this will produce not only certain positive results but also, it appears, unexpected long-term negative effects. Sometimes, intuitive action which appears obvious and logical will increase rather than minimise or remove a difficulty. This is due either to taking an insufficiently overall view of the difference between the beneficial short-term effects and the detrimental long-term effects of measures taken, or because measures and steps are taken in fields which appear to be relevant to the task in hand, but in reality turn out to be irrelevant.

In order to stabilise the world *model*, a move which Forrester presumes must also happen in the *real* world, it was shown that it was not sufficient to affect only a single factor or a small number of factors. Not only must the annual gross capital supply be reduced (by 40 per cent, so that the creation of new capital and the scrapping of the old will balance each other) but also the rate of exploitation of natural resources (75 per cent), disturbances to the environment (50 per cent) and the annual increase in the birthrate.

Forrester keeps returning to the necessity of ensuring that, in the long run, the growth economy must be replaced by a balanced economy in the broadest sense of the term. However, the question of the implications of this for individual firms is generally left unanswered. His balance solution presupposes, however, that the creation of capital for the entire global system can be stabilised, in real terms, at a certain absolute level. Perhaps, in order to draw some sort of conclusion, we can assume that we might be confronted with the demand that a country's total production of goods and services be kept at a fixed price level over a relatively long period of time – in other words, that the annual growth of the gross national product must gradually cease.

If this working hypothesis – and at this stage it can be no more – should ever come about, it would be wrong to interpret it as implying that gradually every company must be forced to stop expanding. Within the concept of constancy there would be room for rapid growth and retrenchment, and long-term stabilisation. It has been said that today almost everything is interrelated. While this is probably true on the whole, it does look as though the degree of mutual dependence is particularly high in certain types of economic system and certain kinds of industries. The surprising but logical consequence of this is that, sooner or later, the extension of any economic parameter inevitably causes a change to occur in other economic parameters at the same or a similar rate. This could result in a great many unforeseen and undesirable consequences. For instance, it might be imagined that the restriction which, "objectively" speaking, a parameter once had – such as the social scope for investments in the energy sector over a two-year period – will by no means correspond to the real limit placed upon it. It might be protests from conservationist groups against the risk of radioactive fall-out from an atomic power station, or about the effect of effluent on ecology, which determine the real limit. This explains to some extent why it is so difficult to be precise about which economic or other units must be stabilised. But the pattern must be reversible, for if growth creates growth, then stagnation will create stagnation. For example, if we should be forced to ration fossil coal on a global scale, this would have undreamed-of adverse repercussions on the motor and petroleum industries, which in their turn would affect the iron and steel industry, the plastic industry, and so on. "We are simply burning up the raw materials needed to make things."

Let us now draw the threads together to form a conclusion. Can the industrial capitalist system adapt itself and continue to function in a stagnating and stabilised economy? If, by "the industrial capitalist system", we mean an economic system in which the right to dispose of a significant proportion of earnings is highly decentralised, and left to a large number of interdependent organisations whose decisions are nevertheless made independently of each other, the answer must be in the negative. The really interesting question, however, is whether we must conclude from this answer that the right to decide on the uses to which profits are to be put must be completely centralised, or whether there is not some intermediate manner in which all the negative effects of increased centralisation could be fairly well balanced against its necessity. It is essential to devote serious thought to this problem. People are demanding a decentralised society in the broadest sense of the term – in other words, a society in which decisions are not made in remote places, far from where they will actually operate; a society free from complex solutions proposed by experts, a society which is not impersonalised and formalised. These demands must be contrasted with what appear to be modern technology's growing requirements for the opposite – large units, a regime of specialists, broad planning, and sophisticated and dehumanised systems of management.

Chapter 7
Qualitative necessity

It is asserted without reservations that we are moving forwards, but "forwards" is only a word, for what does "forwards" mean in this context? Forwards to what?

Ernest Thiel

A company should grow so that there can be a distribution of bonus every other year, but it is of no significance whatever whether it does so by making napalm or tiles.

Sven Fagerberg

The growing criticism of the industrial society and its representatives has many facets. Firms are criticised for rationalising, for using time-and-motion studies, for making employees redundant, for creating a situation in which employees have no right of decision, for poor working conditions, for dishonest advertising, for poor quality products, for a lack of social sense, for cynicism in general and, of course, for trying to make a profit.

One thing which can be said of criticism of this kind is that it is often on the wrong track. The analysis is always extremely vague, and so is its corollary – the generalised statements of industry and business admitting to far-reaching social responsibilities. What does Tore Browaldh, the banker, mean when he states that he clearly realises that a company's responsibility to society goes far beyond the thesis that it simply must make as large a profit as possible?

We can be assured that well-managed companies see the profitability of their own activities as their most important and, indeed, their fundamental guideline. It has been said, and this must be stressed, that the primary objective of a company is to survive; in our economic system this implies making such profit as guarantees the survival of the company, i.e. quite often making maximal profit in the short run. It has also been stressed that every economic system must be able to show a surplus, whether or not this is termed a profit. However, profit is a relative concept, and in order to facilitate the discussion it will be necessary to resort to an analogy. A company's freedom of action is limited externally by those with an interest in it, and internally by the need to survive. The latter need might be seen as a sphere, inside another sphere created by the outside interests, the two concentric units forming a system in constant motion, where their common borders constantly vary and the space between them represents the company's freedom of movement, the space in which it exists.

Those directly concerned, such as society, the employees, the owners, the customers, the directors, the creditors and the competitors, are all interested parties; therefore to some extent their actions determine the framework within which the company has freedom of action. It cannot, for instance, progress at a pace entirely determined by itself. Very high profits, for example, would not only make the shareholders demand higher dividends, but would also result in the employees demanding higher wages. It might transpire, as happens in the USA, that the state would intervene to prevent undesirable growth and the formation of monopolies which sometimes result from too great a profitability. Nevertheless, this external limit, imposed on the independence of the company, is determined even further by all the indirect interactions mentioned above. Profits which at one stage are too high would result in opposition on the part of customers, competitors, and other interested parties at the next stage. The pressure exerted by competition in all its forms will delimit the sphere of interested parties.

The inner limit – the survival sphere – is constituted by parallel factors, and as a concept is much closer to reality. Society makes rules governing such things as liquidation, and the customers make informal minimum limits by, for example, reducing their purchases or showing less good will. No new credits are then made available, there are no deliveries of necessary raw materials, and no influx of new capital will be forthcoming from the shareholders. Taken together, all these factors create an abstract inner limit, and an intuitive conclusion would therefore be that the closer one comes to the survival sphere the more powerful the profit motive becomes.

This analogy helps us to provide something like a reasonable explanation for various ideas and observations. Lord Keynes asserted that he had noticed the tendency of large concerns to socialise themselves. A point is reached in the development of a large company at which the owners of the capital and the management divide into two more or less distinct groups. At this stage the general stability and reputation of the firm are judged more on the quality of the management than on the basis of the shareholders' dividends on their capital. The shareholders must be given a respectable dividend, but once this has been ensured the main interest of the directors is often to avoid criticism from the general public and from their customers. This idea, which was first formulated fifty years ago, has since been developed by many others, and has recently been restated almost without alteration by J. K. Galbraith.

By giving the shareholder a decent annual dividend, by striving to attain a high degree of self-finance and by moving the decision-making process deep into the organisation – where it is out of reach of all outsiders including shareholders – power is kept within the organisation. Some have interpreted this development as a sign that the profit motive is being put aside, which of course is not true. The company adapts itself to the sphere of interested parties and must therefore occasionally be prepared to renounce the criterion of maximum profitability. This does not imply the disappearance of profit as the principal objective, merely that the need to survive has made these changes necessary within the sphere of interested parties. Nor need it be said that dividend policy has no connection with the question of maximising profits. In this respect, it is completely irrelevant whether net profits are kept within the organisation or distributed among the shareholders.

Tore Browaldh maintains that, from his own experience on various boards of directors, he could cite countless examples of occasions where decisions have been made contrary to the narrow concept of profitability and more in the interest of the community. He lists consideration to employees, to a village, to suppliers and to customers as examples.

A number of points must now be raised. Does this mean that the interests of profitability were disregarded for a time, and that the long-term profit making capacity of a company was consciously reduced? Are these companies so dedicated to social and regional policies, and to full employment, that they feel the same sort of responsibility to the community itself and act accordingly? Hardly. This is not how responsibility to the community functions in a business organisation, and this is not how it should function in a capitalist economy.

However, Tore Browaldh is surely sincere in what he says. A partial explanation can be sought in the assumption that the companies concerned were far from the survival sphere. A commercial bank is occasionally forced to write down or write off credits, in order to enable a creditor company to continue; more specifically, it sometimes has to carry the losses of a company over a period of time. Perhaps these are measures which are supposed to be seen as expressions of social responsibility, but there are two important preconditions which must not be forgotten. To begin with, banks are prepared, and indeed are duty-bound, to accept losses of this kind. To have a particularly solid basis and a more-or-less-guaranteed annual profit does not simply mean that the banks can carry temporary burdens, and consequently in this sense find themselves far from the survival sphere, but rather that they can and *must* bear the losses of others. This is their buffer role in the total economy which the community has assigned to its banks, and as a reward they are allowed to keep and to increase their high degree of consolidation. Secondly, the closing of a firm might, in the long run, damage the bank's activities so seriously that they would rather carry a loss than contribute to a bankruptcy. This can scarcely be classified as consideration for the community; on the contrary, it is a matter of acting strictly in accordance with the principle of profitability.

If there is to be any real significance attached to the idea of social responsibility on the part of "big business", then this will only come about when a company which is faced with a choice consciously opts for a course of action leading to higher costs (and/or lower profits) than would accrue from another possible course – *to the extent that the company's survival prospects are palpably diminished.* It seems obvious that the concept can be given no other interpretation. Once this is realised it is much easier to understand why, in contrast to statements of this kind, assertions are made by other leading businessmen to the effect that we should be extremely suspicious of manufacturers or managements who maintain that they are acting in accordance with any principles other than those of business economy.

It appears, then, that it would be extremely difficult to demonstrate that companies in a capitalist economy ever consciously disregard maximal profit as representing their fundamental operational goal and the measure of the efficiency of their activities. The fact that the demand for profit is occasionally given a different name, and might for instance be described as "an increased share of the market", has, in principle, no significance. Temporarily setting aside the demand for the highest possible profit over a given period does not necessarily conflict with long-term striving for maximal profit. It may well be that firms at some distance from the survival sphere will be less concerned with the criterion of profitability, but it is doubtful whether in practice they would also make decisions which would reduce profitability more than necessary and thereby, in any meaningful sense, jeopardise their survival. In other words, to point to a growing sense of social responsibility does not imply that companies have dropped the idea of profitability. It is a case of either maximising profits in another form, or else of a charitable gesture which the company can permit itself since it is well consolidated and generally independent. The third explanation, the only possible one remaining, is that the directors are incompetent.

Can the capitalist system adapt itself qualitatively?

The other question put in the chapter, "A balanced economic system", was whether a developed industrial system, of the type known in the West, could adapt itself *qualitatively* to the demands for a meaningful mode of operations in a decelerating economy. It is highly likely that different demands would be made on the organisation and aims of the company, reflecting the need for a more balanced allocation of resources than is the case in an expanding economy. The specific demands of a balanced economy in this respect can, however, be ignored in the first stage of the discussion.

Quite apart from increasing pressures caused by rapidly dwindling resources, environmental damage and a growing world population, the highly developed industrialised society has certain qualitative difficulties to contend with. There is a crisis of aims, because people or, more precisely, their demands and needs, no longer seem to be considered within the framework of the system we are fashioning.

It is true that such assertions have frequently been made

before. Marx maintained that "production for profit" leads
to production for its own sake without any regard for
mankind's real needs. The next step, he believed, would be
automatic consumption for the sake of consumption, mass
consumption and unnecessary goods. The French socialist
Roger Garaudy points out that Engels' friend, William
Morris, makes the man of the future in the socialist society
say: "We no longer produce for profit but to satisfy needs,
for happiness, for life."

The usual objection to Marx's thesis is that it has often
been convincingly demonstrated that a market system
governed by the expectations of profit is better able to reflect
and cater for needs – as for instance, preferences in household goods – than is possible in a centrally planned economy. Although well-founded, this comment can scarcely
justify asserting that all is as it should be. Criticism is not
necessarily unjustified because the medicine given is either
wrongly prescribed or has a nasty taste.

So long as the individual's ability to influence production
and thereby the pattern of his own consumption is at stake,
we cannot be convinced of the truth either of apologetic or
"explanatory" statements that the power of the consumer is
intact, or of an economist's complex assurances that we are
living in the best of all possible worlds. Usually it is the
intellectual who is most articulate in expressing his dissatisfaction; he argues that, in the world of free industrial
activity, it is obviously possible to initiate the production of
absolutely anything – "A gadget, perfumed lavatory paper,
or toy bazookas: any gimmick from which you can earn
money, and you don't care a damn whether your brainwave
leads to something which is necessary. . . . At no stage do
you take part in any real planning on the basis of people's
needs, society's needs (which are, or should be, the same
thing)."

Examples and questions can be extended to almost any
area in the production of goods and services, and this forms
the basis for criticism. Nevertheless, it is the system as a

whole which is wrong, and it would be short-sighted and probably ineffective to concentrate on details. What people think they know often has very little connection with reality. The way things actually are and the way they appear to be are not necessarily identical: this has meant, among other things, that the responsibility for some development of which many people disapprove is ascribed to the wrong reasons or the wrong people. In reality, for instance, there is very little scope for criticising an individual company or branch for "manipulating" the consumer. To make lavatory paper double and thereby double the turnover (which actually happened) is a brilliant idea which is undoubtedly an excellent example of successful market manipulation. If a margarine manufacturer sells his product with varying amounts of salt and degrees of hardness and fat content, the butter manufacturers will naturally be compelled to produce a similar variety. Criticism of the firms concerned is unjustified, or at any rate pointless. In practice, how can Swedish industry evolve its own approach or pay attention to the consumer's needs and wishes when to do this is bound to reduce its own profitability? In this respect it has no significant freedom of movement whatsoever.

The sense of distaste felt by most people at the choice of products and the distribution of resources in modern society is, however, connected with everyday experience. One could ask in whose interest thirty-seven different detergents are manufactured: the consumer's? everyone's? Some people think that one would be enough. However, the analysis can be taken further. The market for household goods in Sweden is expanded by some fifteen hundred new products every year. In a well-stocked departmental store there are perhaps six hundred articles today which were not there a year ago. The addition of so many new lines each year must obviously tie vast resources to development, production and distribution – even without making anything but marginal changes such as in packaging, appearance and so on. This has already been referred to as "pseudo-development". If

instead of twenty kinds of toothpaste we were content with a
choice of five, the accumulation of capital in the distribution
trade would inevitably be far smaller. The question would
then have to be asked, how many local and small rural shops
have been forced to close down because they have been
unable to find and/or pay interest on the capital tied to an
unnecessarily large variety of products? If it is an unhealthy
situation when, on the one hand, capital is confined to
certain goods and services which, "objectively" speaking,
are unnecessary (without any further restrictions than those
created by the credit and capital market) while, on the other,
the lack of capital in, for example, the public sector
(hospitals, education, etc.) is making itself felt in many
countries. The fact that these two sectors are independent of
each other does not affect the criticism in principle.

No distinction is made in intrinsic value between product
$_1$ and product $_2$. Seen through the eyes of the market system
everything is equally justified. The freedom to advertise
alcohol is just as great as the freedom to advertise fruit juice,
to manufacture cigarettes as great as to wash shirts. Silver
champagne whisks, electric toothbrushes, barbecue knives
and countless other useless implements are all manufactured, while kidney machines, artificial limbs for the physically handicapped and sewage systems which will not
damage the environment are in short supply.

These are far more serious accusations than anything
which can be levelled at the faults in the consumer goods
sector, and these have far more drastic consequences. Not
even the most well-founded refusal to contemplate the idea
of a centrally directed economy can excuse lack of criticism
of the imperfections and faults of the capitalist system when
it comes to the criteria governing the choice of products. At
the moment, there are both criticisms and suggestions for
improvement in circulation, but faulty premises abound.

There are, however, certain grounds for caution and
moderation in this criticism. It is clear that all knowledge,
every product and every service can be utilised for a purpose

different from that for which it is originally produced. A knife can be used for eating, but it can also be a deadly weapon. Although James Watson's and Francis Crick's epoch-making definition of the DNA molecule's structure offers long-term prospects such as the choice of a child's sex, raising the level of intelligence and extending people's working lives, these future perspectives, which intuitively and at first sight appear to be positive, could be turned against mankind, or at least against certain groups of people. There are countless similar examples. The fact that so many intellectuals today appear to be profoundly concerned with the question of man's own responsibility and the innate evil and aggression within him can, perhaps, be seen in this context.

This important reservation aside, there are other reasons for looking more closely at the mistaken priorities and misuse of resources which, as more and more people are beginning to realise, are evident in the industrial, capitalist society. It is tempting to accept the positivist's tolerance of misery, waste and evil as the price we have to pay for all the good things around us. But this kind of evasion of the problem should not be allowed when the pollution of our air and our water is almost total, when stocks of atomic weapons are sufficient to exterminate us all several times over and when we have at the most 150 years before the resources of fossil coal, perhaps the most important factor in modern society, are exhausted.

The unfortunate consequences of liberalism

Before we investigate this problem in greater depth, it is important to comment on the historical background. When they were first formulated, the fundamental ideas behind the market system were radical in comparison with the narrow ideas, sectarianism and system of economic privilege which had been the hallmarks of feudalism and merchant capitalism. The aim of liberalism, which expresses the ideas of the market system, is ideologically and economically to live and let live, to allow people the freedom to say and do what they wish; it seeks tolerance, so far as the need for public order permits, and criticises the unjust system of economic wealth. In the historical context, this ideology adapted to its contemporary social atmosphere. Bertrand Russell was of the opinion that liberalism, in the widest sense of the term, is a product of trade. Trade, he believed, brings men into contact with people who have different cultures from their own, and this serves to undermine the dogmatism which characterises the inexperienced.

John Stuart Mill is perhaps the principal liberal ideologist. His writings of more than a hundred years ago (he died in 1873) demonstrate an enviable amount of wisdom, radicalism and understanding of the current situation. The ideas of economic freedom he propounded had, however, been formulated by others long before. Adam Smith's famous book, *The Wealth of Nations*, was published as early as 1776, and in it Smith emerged as the spokesman for free trade.[8] He maintained that the state should only have three tasks – to defend the nation against foreign enemies, to maintain a legal system and to ensure the construction and maintenance of transport systems. In other words, it should deal with those tasks which it would be unprofitable for individuals to undertake themselves. In addition, it was assumed that some unspecified supernatural power, an "invisible hand", would regulate business life so that undesirable phenomena disappeared of their own accord.

The basis of the argument was that the same order and harmony hold sway in economic life as in nature. It was believed that the distribution of resources would regulate itself according to quite simple laws. Goods and services for which there was a demand would be produced and put at the disposal of the consumer, and prices would regulate themselves according to the principles of supply and demand. Attracted by greater profits and rewards, capital and labour would, more or less of their own accord, move wherever there was a demand and move away again once the market was saturated.

It was believed that the economic system could maintain this harmony only as long as it was shielded from any unjustified and artificial influence, and in particular against state interference. Economic life represented a part of nature, and any unnecessary intervention in its well-regulated and balanced development would affect the natural laws governing it.

The liberal economic ideas were not, however, put into practice until much later, and in England only after 1830. Liberalism's best-known concrete contribution concerned trade policy, in particular the move towards free trade of which the corn laws were the most famous example. Free trade, and thereby the market system, spread throughout Europe in the period 1830–70, but it never became as extensive as its proponents had hoped. Eli F. Heckscher even believes that liberalism's influence on the system of customs-dues has been somewhat exaggerated.

The rather limited progress of economic liberalism is worth investigating more closely. How did it come about that the ideas and the political-economical programme – which seemed the most appropriate course of action given the contemporary situation – did not generally assert themselves as they deserved? To understand this we must first analyse the economic development of Britain between 1750 and 1850. There are two particularly important factors apparent in the developing industry of the country: (1) the degree of interdependence in the industrial system; and (2) the related question of the size of the company.

In this respect Adam Smith noted two essential points. To begin with, industrial production in the eighteenth century was dominated by cottage industry, i.e., production was carried out in small units, more often than not as an additional occupation in the home. The worker owned the means of production, while the merchant capitalist owned the capital required to buy the raw materials. There were no compelling reasons for the various units to work together economically – on the contrary, individualism seems to have been the order of the day. Even by the end of the eighteenth century, the factory system whereby numbers of workers are gathered under one roof had not yet caught on.

Secondly, Adam Smith noted that even in his day companies were generally small, the only exception to this rule being the trading companies which, at the height of the mercantilist period before 1690, had been given concessions in a number of geographical areas for trading in certain categories of goods.

The important feature, however, was the fact that the large business monopolies were losing their position of strength by the end of the eighteenth century. The British East India Company, which had been founded in 1600 and had accumulated enormous profits by the end of the seventeenth century, thus making its owners the richest men in England, went into decline. In 1813 the trade monopoly with India was abolished and, in 1833, trade with China was similarly thrown open to all. By 1858 the East India Company had gone into liquidation and ceased to exist – a development accurately predicted by Adam Smith.

Business life around 1830, and in the previous decades, was characterised by small companies which were more or less independent of each other and made little attempt to co-operate – an "atomistic" society in the true meaning of the word. Only because of the increasing extent to which home industries were being supplanted by centralised production in factories, could it be said that the structure of business life was in any way different from that which existed around 1750.

The conclusion must be that the line of thought represented by Adam Smith and John Stuart Mill is understandable and justifiable given its historical background. A free market in goods and services was natural, and doubtless an effective means of regulating an atomistic market. The same

was true of freedom of thought and expression, and Mill
could scarcely have foreseen the oligo-political character
which the media have since acquired.

After 1830, however, something happened which had a
profound significance for the efficient functioning of this type
of society: the manufacturing units grew in size and became
much more interdependent. The atomistic society which
Adam Smith had foreseen, and which John Stuart Mill had
presupposed, was beginning to vanish. This was initially
because the great economic significance of the railways was
becoming apparent at this time. The railway companies
were   forced   into   extensive   co-operation   and   co-
ordination – developments primarily determined by a need
for capital of a completely different order from anything
previously experienced. Indirectly, the building of the railways stimulated the formation of credit institutions and the
concept of the limited company, but at the same time the
ease of transport had, by definition, a cohesive effect. The
most important of the changes set in motion was the inevitability of monopolies.

The years immediately following 1830 are characterised
by a rapid growth in the size of manufacturing companies –
at this point one can talk of a "take-off" for size variables.
While cottage industry was the dominant mode of production, the production units had been small. A large textile
industry around 1830 seldom employed more than 1,500
workers, and the largest iron foundries had, perhaps, as
many as 2,000 employees. A well-known exception was a
combined spinning and weaving mill which is said to have
employed about 7,000 workers. However, one exponent of
the new trend was the German firm of Krupp, founded at
the beginning of the nineteenth century. At first it had
grown at a slow pace, only employing 700 workers in 1851,
but after this the numbers grew rapidly, reaching 2,000 only
ten years later in 1861 and 16,000 by 1873. By this time
Krupps were probably the largest firm in Europe, though
not the only company to have undergone a similar develop-

ment. In short, the period after 1830 was characterised by
the transition from medium-sized, highly individualised textile mills to large-scale heavy industry with strong ties
between the different branches. In this new situation, the
individualist idea that a firm could adapt its production to
the changing preferences of the market without any particular preparation was less convincing.

These developments also meant that the basis of economic
liberalism – the fragmented society with absolutely free
competition – had disappeared. The gradual dilution and
diminishing practicability of liberal ideas can only be
properly understood if the changed conditions are made
clear. Indeed, liberal economic doctrines have also gradually
been altered – often to such an extent that they are now
scarcely recognisable.

The freedom of a company to produce and sell as much as
it wishes, to carry on its activities where and when it pleases
and according to whatever methods it cares to choose, has
already been limited and, more significantly, shows signs of
being restricted still further. In almost every field, freedom
of action on the part of companies has been circumscribed
by the community and by other interested parties. There is,
however, one exception – within the framework of the
resources available, companies are essentially at liberty to
produce *whatever* they want.

In principle there is a clear similarity between the
freedom for a company to pay the wages it wants on the one
hand, and to develop, manufacture and sell whatever
product it wishes on the other. However, although in the
first instance its freedom is severely limited by the system of
wage negotiations, in the second it is largely unrestricted. It
is not a qualitatively different freedom, since the idea was
that free competition should regulate both wages and the
choice of products. It was considered that only those goods
or services permitted by the principle of natural selection
(i.e. the law of supply and demand) would come on to the
market and establish a position. Perhaps this worked in the

atomistic society, as for example in Britain between 1800 and 1870, but mainly because it was an imperfect society. Even if the forces of the free market were put out of action, there was still an unsatiated demand for utilities, in the real meaning of the word, which could profitably be provided for. The situation is different in an affluent society, not in the sense that there are no suitable areas where needs can be fulfilled, but rather because the low degree of profitability in many of them diverts production resources to sectors which are already well provided and where the prospect of profit is judged to be better.

The trade union movement, employment legislation, nature conservancy bodies, bank inspection and consumer protection, are all representatives of the forces which complement or limit those of the free market. Almost without exception, the regulations are concerned with spheres other than the area of production in which the firm is engaged. Admittedly, there are some products which companies are not allowed to manufacture without restriction, such as certain poisons and preparations endangering the environment or the individual, and explosives; but the numbers involved are small and of little significance in comparison with total production. Most products in the private sector have been manufactured purely because the company judged that, in the prevailing situation, these were the most likely to be profitable. On the whole, companies in a capitalist system are still free to make whatever they please, the only limitations being on how, where and when they do it, and in some cases what they do with the product following manufacture. The forces of the free market have been limited and balanced in virtually all areas except the one which could justifiably be considered the most important.

This everlasting tolerance on the part of the community should be seen as a sign that the most fundamental aspect of liberalism is still alive and can still assert itself. The weakness of liberalism is that, because of the way in which it functions, it never makes a judgement as to whether or not the aims or actions of a company are justified. The choice must be made on the basis of the natural order of things, which, in an economic context, is the same as saying that any product or service which can be sold – and sold at a profit – is justified. The same is true of the choice of ideas: only opinions for which there is a demand are likely to survive.

To refuse to listen to an opinion because of your certainty that it is wrong is to assume that your own ideas are based on absolute truth, argues John Stuart Mill, and he is of course right. But in the case of both freedom of trade and freedom of thought it should be remembered that neither Smith nor Mill were faced with the enormous development-potential of a large firm, with its vast manufacturing resources and almost irresistible power to lead the market in any direction, or with the influence of modern mass-media, but merely with a community of small, independent institutions which were competing with each other on an equal footing.

There is, to put it mildly, a considerable difference between resorting to violence in an emergency, and the systematic use by the state of the most sophisticated technological methods of annihilation. Likewise there is a vast gap between the right of a small firm to work with whatever it chooses, and the freedom of a multinational organisation to develop, manufacture and sell anything that it wishes. A refusal to see or to distinguish between qualitatively different firms, actions, or aims is the most negative contribution made by liberalism and, unfortunately, the one which has survived the longest. It is fundamentally this which explains our unwillingness, up to now, to attempt to govern the aims of companies and thereby society's production of goods and services in general.

Reaction – or adaptation?

The sheer number of areas in which we suspect a false distribution of resources is sufficient to lead to the conclusion that immediate action is imperative. If, in addition, we list the particular demands on the distribution of resources which will inevitably be made in an economy where the raw materials needed for production are not only becoming scarcer but the demands for resources on the part of the consumers are also growing, there is every reason to wonder how a more balanced allocation of resources can possibly be achieved within the framework of the industrial capitalist system.

In principle there are only two possible alternatives – to either re-establish the conditions in which the liberal concept can operate or consciously adapt to change. The first solution, the attempt to re-create the conditions prevailing when the *laissez-faire* system was developed in the eighteenth and nineteenth centuries, would not only require halting the apparently irreversible trend towards increasingly large companies and a greater interdependence of units within the economic system, but would also demand that the present business structure should be disintegrated.

The anti-trust policies in the USA at the turn of the century aimed at achieving just such a situation as this. Such moves are understandable given the trend towards combines and monopolies, which was probably more pronounced at that time than ever before or since. From about 1875 to 1904, two hundred different companies with a capital of a million dollars or more had been formed, and they controlled about 40 per cent of the total capital resources of American industry. Standard Oil owned 90 per cent of the petroleum industry, American Tobacco 90 per cent of the tobacco industry and similar situations prevailed in the fields of agricultural machinery, steel and cane sugar.

Most historians agree that the anti-trust movement has

been far from successful, and the history of Standard Oil illustrates this particularly well. When the Standard Oil Trust was formed in 1882 it controlled between 90 and 95 per cent of refined petroleum production in the USA. As a legal institution the Trust merely meant that the shares in a number of competing firms were gathered together into the same hands by being exchanged for what were known as "Trust certificates"; these admittedly gave their owners access to dividends, but at the same time deprived them of their voting rights and thereby of any influence on the movement. The State of Ohio started legal proceedings and demanded that the Trust should exclude all shares in Standard Oil Co. of Ohio, which at that time was one of forty-one companies making up the Trust. It was maintained that this particular company had operated against public interest by becoming associated with the Trust, which could only be considered as a monopoly and therefore in conflict with current legislation. The court's judgement went against Standard Oil Trust, after which other States also prepared similar proceedings, and the usefulness of the Trust as a means of keeping the various components together came to an end. It was officially dissolved in 1892, only to be replaced by Standard Oil Co. of New Jersey, which as a holding company (formally, but not in essence, different from a trust) was in more or less complete control of the American oil empire. The relative defeat of the anti-trust policy is, on the basis of conditions prevailing at the time, scarcely surprising – it would have been more surprising had it succeeded.

These setbacks and difficulties have not prevented similar ideas from reappearing, some of which have a bearing on the present situation. There is also a romantic and somewhat naïve hope that it might be possible, by means of a determined policy, to replace the large companies of today with small units spread throughout the country and preferably operated on a co-operative basis. Alongside this rather unrealistic idea there are other more traditional and scientific concepts which argue in favour of disintegrating the larger companies. Certain costs occasioned by planning, direction and the administrative superstructure have been absorbed by the extremely rapid expansion achieved almost universally by the large firms; these are costs which in a less expansive situation would become more obvious and militate in favour of a breakdown into smaller units. From a different standpoint, Assar Lindbeck argues that losses in efficiency would not necessarily be particularly dramatic if large American companies were divided into units between a fifth and a tenth of their present size. He adds, however, that for a small country like Sweden, the possibilities inherent in dividing companies into smaller units without serious loss of efficiency are probably far less.

However, neither the idea of planned growth nor the doubts and possibilities expressed from various quarters can be said to have had any tangible effect on the trend towards further growth. There are, meanwhile, a few people seriously trying to re-create the main conditions necessary for a re-establishment of the *laissez-faire* pattern. Though fundamentally a reactionary solution, a return to the old state of affairs might well be considered by some as one of the two classical ways out of a difficult situation. The other way out – a radical adaptation to new conditions – is the one which history has shown to be nearly always successful in the long run. Presumably, this will be proved so yet again.

What must be the basis of the new thinking? What is implied by "a radical adaptation"?

Expressed briefly, we must question the firmly established principle of a company's freedom to act as it wishes, that is to say, the more or less unrestricted right of the directors and management to distribute their profits for further development or for expansion, as they themselves find most fitting.

The criticism of multinational companies can be said to touch on three essentially different problems. Firstly, they

are criticised for trying to establish themselves where wages
are lowest, to borrow money where it is cheapest and to take
their profits where taxes are lowest. These criticisms are
voiced particularly by politicians and trade unionists and
are occasioned by the idea that powerful international organisations are run and controlled by means which, from a
national viewpoint, are unsatisfactory. Secondly, it is argued
that the tendency towards monopolising the market, which
is often a facet of international companies, is unfortunate and
should be opposed. The relative inefficiency of huge concerns is also criticised. In this last respect it is possible to
discern not only the idea that this type of large industrial
concern is bound to incur increased costs which have not yet
been realised, but also the rather less well-defined feeling
that a large concern will create costs, resulting either from
its impersonal nature, or from malaise amongst its employees. These costs cannot be measured, yet they are there
and have to be paid for by the organisation's employees.

A more subtle criticism, which can be placed in the third
category, argues that the very size of these companies con-
stitutes a potential, or even an actual, threat. The largest
multinational companies allocate such huge resources that
only the governments of a handful of countries can ever
aspire to having so much at their disposal. Moreover,
decisions are taken by directors who are inaccessible to
outsiders – therefore out of the public eye, and immune
from the influences which would normally be exercised
when there is a case of extreme concentration of power.

It is particularly difficult to feel much sympathy with
criticism of the first kind, which is rooted in the limitations
of the national state. Is it not true that the multinational
companies are helping to break down the characteristic
self-centredness of states, which today is not only a
common but also a dangerous anachronism? (A desire to see
the gradual disappearance of the national state should not, as
so often happens, be taken as a desire to obliterate linguistic,
cultural and other ethnic characteristics.)

The tendencies towards domination of the market, and the other forms of monopolisation which inevitably result from the growth of multinational companies, are not necessarily bad nor should they be opposed under present circumstances. Size, as such, cannot, in the modern world, be said to be unreasonable or undesirable. It is the way in which this size is used that should be questioned. Suppose we imagine that the two biggest industrial concerns in the world devoted all their enormous energies – development potential, manufacturing resources and market techniques – to areas where action was most needed: to famine, sickness, environmental damage or the problems of urbanisation, instead of to space projects, supersonic aeroplanes, military technology or luxury consumer goods, as they do now. Would we then be so inclined to criticise these firms for being too powerful, inefficient, inflexible or generally unethical? This is hardly likely. Obviously, it does not imply that there are no disadvantages in large industrial concerns, only that those disadvantages usually cited are more related to what a firm is doing than merely to its size.

In the unique present-day situation where global, technically complicated and administratively difficult problems must be solved, the organisation which has access to large-scale technical development and production capacity, and also possesses an international management and control system, will be a valuable asset. However, the multinational companies will only become assets if they show their willingness to co-operate, with all that this entails as seen from the company viewpoint – renunciation of power, a limitation on freedom and stagnation. Unfortunately, the likelihood of this happening is slender; it would be contrary to every historical precedent and to all the indications provided by the way in which our economic system works.

A leading Swedish businessman, basing his opinion on his own observations, has argued that the multinational companies not only aim to make a profit, but have also taken social responsibilities upon themselves. Unless the concept is diluted to such a degree that it becomes practically meaningless, this obviously cannot be true. One can only doubt whether international companies could ever create a new and more humane society by the usual methods of continued expansion. Such an approach can only result in the formation of a society similar, in almost all respects, to the one which we now feel it necessary to reject – though with even more "gigantomania", more unnecessary gimmicks forced on us by increasingly subtle and powerful marketing techniques, and an even greater imbalance between those who "have" and those who "have not". Nor can we leave the global problems of resources and the environment to the multinational companies, and imagine they will be solved. As long as some attractive raw material is available and can be exploited without any other limitations than those created by the market, then it will undoubtedly be exploited. As long as there is a place where it is possible to establish a factory which can spew forth poisonous vapours or polluted air without restrictions, then this site will be chosen in preference to an equally suitable position where such things are prohibited. "Social responsibility" is merely an expression which can be used and abused at whim. It is important to realise that, like any other company in the capitalist economic system, the multinational companies do not take upon themselves any social responsibility which is not subordinate to the long-term demand for profits.

The Utopia for representatives of the multinational companies and for the directors of international organisations is a world government, a world without boundaries. "Absolute freedom to move people, goods, ideas, services and capital. No armies, no fleets. Only local police. A single global system for patents and trademarks, for building and security regulations. One food standard, one global currency, one single central bank."

Is this not, though, a distorted vision which should be seen as nothing more than an extension of the current problems and desires of large concerns? Is it certain that this imaginary world government's far-reaching demands for information, consultation and a share of profits, which would doubtless be made if the vision became reality, are also on the list of desiderata?

One thing is clear. If we wish to create resources to help us not only to solve the most pressing global problems but also to avoid an undesirable allocation of what we have at present, and to provide instead an approach more appropriate to real needs, there must be certain restrictions on the freedom of any firm to allocate its profits as it thinks fit. The right of the huge internationalised companies to use their net profits as they wish, and to distribute investments in subsidiaries and in spheres which they consider most profitable, must be controlled. As before, the community must undertake the task of reducing the present freedom of companies, but this time the community should not only be considered in the sense of the individual nation, but also as the community in a supra-national sense. This is an essential foundation for even attempting to undertake the task.

It must be an absolute condition that strict limitations be placed on the capitalist system's built-in tolerance, which enables it to allow innocuous, essential and uncontroversial goods and services to be produced side by side, and on an equal footing, with destructive, superfluous, and, in the general view, undesirable products. A pound profit on product $_1$ is not necessarily as valuable as a pound profit on product $_2$. This is worth shouting from the rooftops.

Can there be any justification for failure to discriminate against some action which most people find evil, unjust or unacceptable? Many who believe there can, base their argument on the classical motivation that it is impossible to make an "objective" decision as to what is evil, unjust or unacceptable; someone will always suffer. By extending this point of view we understand why there is so much opposition to increased democratic control, not least in respect of the management of a manufacturing company. Nevertheless, such control is inevitable: it is a qualitative necessity.

The emerging picture of a future economic system makes it clear that the individual company's freedom of action will be further curtailed. Progress towards a balance cannot fail to lead to a redistribution of the incomes and fortunes associated with business life, which will be based on criteria quite different from those prevailing today. It is difficult to see how society can avoid taking control of an even greater share of companies' incomes. If the annual growth finally disappears, as we must presume it will, the resources necessary for what will undoubtedly be a costly process of reorganisation, and for the even more expensive survival phase, can only be created by means of a completely new and ruthless redistribution of resources and assets. New rules and instruments for redistribution must be created, and in many essential respects these will redefine and restrict the present main rule – the criterion of profit – which guides the distribution of resources in the capitalist, economic system.

The next question which must be asked is, does all this mean socialism?

Chapter 8
A programme and a vision

It is not the difference between the United States and the Soviet Union which should worry us, but what they have in common. . . . These technocrats, who consider themselves to be opponents, are both dragging mankind in the same direction, towards the destruction of true humanity.

François Mauriac

It appears as if we are faced with two different problems – what *must* be done and what *should* be done.

What we must do, in the short run, is to continue to adapt ourselves to the rules of technology, which no economic forces or political ideology can (or will) alter. These are the guidelines and conditions which force us towards even more rationalisation, systematisation, calculation and planning, and which mean that the organisation and distribution of work must be based on far-reaching divisions, one-sidedness and regular profits. There are no exceptions to these demands in any developed economy, whether it calls itself "mixed" or "socialist".

What makes the present situation so unattractive is that the prospect before us is not one of diminishing central planning, smaller organisations, decreasing specialisation and efficiency, but one in which these faults are multiplied. There is then no other way out if we are to use technology in solving the crisis of shortages as well as maintaining a high material standard. Nor is that all – it seems that, at this stage, there is no opportunity to choose a different form of

society, even if we should wish to do so, since the effects of
the industrial way of life are probably such as to make
survival impossible unless we first compensate Nature for
centuries of careless treatment. It is really an absurd
situation that a growing proportion of industry's resources
are now devoted to producing means of remedying the
effects of its earlier behaviour, and to preventing further
offences. What was not profitable when it should have been,
has now become profitable when it ought not to be so.

In a further discussion of this subject it might be worthwhile to distinguish between what must be done, in the
short run, with the co-operation of advanced technology and
the highly industrialised social order, as distinct from the
hypothetical future situation in which people will be free to
organise both their work and their society as a whole.

At the end of the last chapter the question was posed as to
whether the present situation would inevitably lead to
socialism. If we follow Lenin's concept of socialism as it is
usually understood, i.e. that the state will take over the
means of production, we have every reason to believe that
this process alone will neither solve the problem nor offer a
ready-made programme of action.

This purely practical observation does not constitute a
rejection of socialism in principle – on the contrary, private
control of vast resources is wrong. People today are more
collectivised than ever before. What they are able to achieve
is less the result of their own hard work than of everything
which is placed at their disposal by an accumulation of
knowledge and experience, by the environment and by the
community. The same is true of their organised activities
and initiatives. As has been shown, the far-sighted manufacturer who exploits some invention may have made only a
marginal contribution to its realisation, but because of
technological advantages and legal protection he is able to
extract most of the profit from it. Is this right? There is
really only a difference of degree between this example and
that of the doctor who earns £15,000 a year by treating

people with preparations in the development and distribution of which he has played no part.

The most elementary knowledge of history shows clearly
that ownership of this kind is a fairly modern phenomenon,
and in no way something which cannot be changed or, as
people often seem to think, which has been ordained by
God. The idea that the means of production are anyone's
private property, to be used or not used according to
whether or not the owner could profit from it, was not, for
example, an accepted principle in England under the
Tudors or Stuarts. At that time, possession of the means of
production involved a responsibility to others which was not
directly related to the profitability of business economy. It
was only after the expulsion of the Stuart dynasty in 1688
that these rights of ownership were established.

The view of Marx and other nineteenth-century socialists,
that individual ownership hindered the achievement of the
socialist society with full and meaningful employment for all
citizens, must also be seen in this context, though it had
other and more down-to-earth reasons as well. The distribution of income in society was still extremely unfair. On the
one hand, a great many farmers and workers were living at
subsistence level, while, on the other, the incomes of business
companies were often so great that they themselves were
able to finance rapid expansion. In a representative balance
sheet from the middle of the nineteenth century, the firm's
own capital was responsible for perhaps 80 per cent of total
assets, while the corresponding figure today would be a mere
20 per cent. The enormous differences in the level of
consumption and the miserable working conditions of the
ordinary people, and, more important, the possibility of
identifying large incomes, relative luxury and all the
negative sides of the industrial society with certain individuals or families, should be seen as a reasonable explanation as to why rationalisation was seen as the only way to
create a socialist society.

Today the situation is different. The ownership of the

means of production by the state, local authorities or co-operative ventures changes nothing in itself. In principle, ownership by the community does not conflict with the idea of a market economy in a capitalist sense, and it certainly does not make it impossible. (Market socialism can be said to be an intermediate form based on this simple observation.) Only if we aim to completely centralise profits, or to take over the means of payment and replacement, have we created a new form of society, though scarcely a better form if, in all essential aspects, we continue to exploit our resources in the same way as in a market economy. For example, there would be a need for a central planning apparatus which, despite determined work and vast resources, would be unlikely to even remotely approach the planning efficiency possible under a more decentralised system.

Of course it is possible to nationalise certain branches of heavy industry, a move which is seen as politically opportune. However, nothing would be changed fundamentally even if all major concerns were nationalised – simply because all these undertakings are already nationalised in practice if not in theory. Marx foresaw this development, and maintained that the fragmentation of a large concern's own capital among thousands of shareholders really betokens a breaking down of private ownership. This practical implication of the way in which the developed industrial society functions has subsequently been emphasised and further discussed by numerous writers – Alan Harrington, James Burnham, Ernst Wigforss and others. Alan Harrington, for instance, asks what strange process of self-deception makes us consider our firms to be private. We are in the midst of a development in which old ideas on ownership and the owner's function are being changed, argues Ernst Wigforss. But that is not all: in certain important spheres a new type of society is being created where new methods of reconciling the demand for equality and efficiency can emerge.

There is no reserve of ideologically suited, well trained and experienced economists and technologists who could take over and run the complicated technical and economic system represented by a highly developed industrial society. By and large, the same people with the same values would probably be manning the system whether it was in private or state ownership. To propose the nationalisation of large companies as a method of solving our immediate problems is merely to play with trivialities.

What, then, should be our attitude towards small, privately owned companies? Should they not be taken over by the community and run on a co-operative basis? The question should be approached from the opposite angle: we should instead ask whether we need small and medium-sized businesses alongside the really large ones. The answer must be a categorical "yes". The phenomena which the nineteenth-century socialists attacked most vehemently were the inhuman consequences of the rational society created by big industrial enterprises, while Marx, for instance, spoke with some understanding of smaller trades and industries. It is an ironic paradox that variations in the production methods of large industries are relatively few, whether they are in developed socialist or capitalist economies; the principal contrast is the fact that all capitalist – as opposed to socialist – societies contain numerous small and medium-sized businesses alongside the larger concerns. To kill off small firms, with their frequent high degree of flexibility, low administrative costs, willingness to attempt innovations and more humane milieu, is probably one of the most costly mistakes made by the socialist economies.

The original small manufacturer, the pioneer who embarks on a fairy-tale career with empty hands and a head full of ideas, is an asset in any community. Making such initiatives impossible can never be called socialism. On the contrary, it represents a disservice to socialism to make it impossible to dispose of one's means of production by selling them, enabling others to inherit them, or giving them to someone else without strict limitations or the approval of the community.

So it would seem that conventional socialism cannot be expected to offer a suitable programme for action. No difficulties will really be removed by the creation of a socialist society. Lenin felt that the first requirement, necessary to ensure that the initial phase of the communist society was successful, was "registration and inspection which can be done by everyone able to read or write". Reality is, however, different. The state bureaucracy in every developed socialist economy appears to be vast and cumbersome: its most important daily task, which makes the greatest demand on its resources, is to maintain the short-term balance between supply and demand for every commodity. "The major part of all planning in a centrally directed economy is devoted to doing what market mechanisms achieve without difficulty." The demiurgic trait which is often found in socialism seems, on reflection, to lack any real foundation.

There is, of course, even less reason to have any confidence in those who prescribe the consolidation of a pluralistic society with widespread decentralised freedom. This is the old liberal point of view which can most easily be dismissed by merely looking around and deciding whether or not things should continue as they are now. One solution which is intuitively felt to be frustrating, but which is really quite obvious, is that the optimal short-term effect (not to be confused with what our ultimate aim should be) should lie somewhere between the two extremes – the centrally planned socialist economy and the developed mixed economy upon which the form of society sometimes termed social-liberal is based.

What is to be done? What phenomena should be dealt with first of all? What will be the consequences for industry and for the individual firm? Which freedoms must be limited?

Some indication can be found in the analysis already

carried out. It would appear that progress governs man, rather than the reverse as it should be. However, this is not a question of some supernatural, predetermined form of progress. Nor is man being driven by the profound and powerful forces of a progressive urge, by curiosity or the longing for material things. In fact it is unlikely that he can be commanded to resort to overdevelopment. The explanation is not to be found in the impulses deriving from some dynamic qualities in reality itself, but is probably to be sought instead in the image of reality upon which man is to base his actions.

The fact that a certain way of organising work, coupled with an interaction between the image and reality itself, gradually creates an increasingly high material standard nevertheless cannot intrinsically be seen as negative or undesirable. It only becomes so when we either believe we have sufficient material things, which is scarcely likely to happen, or else discover that further material production is impossible because the resources are almost exhausted, when the manner of production and social conditions become difficult to accept or the negative effects in general are clearly felt. That point has virtually been reached now, and we are discovering to our amazement that the image refuses to allow its "will to progress" to be slowed down or stopped. However, if we say – as we are inclined to do – that economic forces are in control, it is also easy though incorrect to ascribe the responsibility for developments to current reality, often to a particular person, instead of to the image. It is escapism to blame "the capitalists", "them" or "ICI": all are the willing servants of the image.

Politicians' freedom of action is equally circumscribed. There is a disturbing and symptomatic parallel in the positions in which government ministers, industry and commerce and the directors of large concerns find themselves. In the present world situation, what real chance has a country like Sweden to choose a radically different commercial policy? None whatever. We are forced to adapt to the parameters of the world around us, whether or not they are based on norms and conditions which we find acceptable. As the Swedish Minister of Finance argues, with a touch of despondency, every year we become more and more closely tied to the international economy, the development of which is dominated by the view of economic questions current in the world at large, ". . . and those views are unfortunately not in accordance with social democratic thinking." Another typical remark made by a Swedish government politician is that the conflict between what we know would be to Sweden's advantage as well as being morally right, and the possibility of asserting ourselves in a world increasingly dominated by competition, is a question to which there is no answer.

The lack of freedom, of which these responsible politicians are aware, is obviously not associated solely with one party or one person. Irrespective of whether we have a right-wing or left-wing government, its representatives would essentially be tied to the international pattern of development. In fact the statesmen of all countries find themselves in the same position of dependence whether they represent a capitalist or socialist society.

A recent report published by the Canadian Senate's research committee reviews the potential of modern technology in both a positive and negative sense. The committee notes that action must be taken to stop uncontrolled developments, then makes the revealing but predictable reservation that a country like Canada should not be too pessimistic simply because the global situation seems to be heading in a dangerous direction. There is no need to panic, to throw research and development overboard or to renounce a share in the benefits ensuing from them. The obvious implication is that "something must be done" provided Canada does not have to do it!

Government politicians are like business managers in a kind of market system where, under present conditions, their own company must expand and be rationalised like any

industrial concern. Without constant growth in the production of goods and services no Western politician in recent
years would have been able to achieve the demand for a high
standard of living and for reforms capable of maintaining his
own country's international competitiveness. Nevertheless,
expansion alone is insufficient, for the firm must be rationalised and developed politically and economically. Re-
training schemes, adult education and leisure policies are
good examples of rationalisation at this level. Centralised
computer records were a successful innovation. A first
precondition for being allowed to retain their place in the
political leadership is never to be less competent than their
foreign colleagues in maintaining their own country's international sales potential. Equally compelling factors are the
constant introduction of new measures and greater efficiency
into society.

The image of economic reality which we have created has
progressively reduced the individual firm's room for manoeuvre. However deeply disturbed a manufacturer might be
by the direction which developments are taking, he must
suppress his sense of danger if his company is to survive.
Likewise the political system has further limited politicians'
freedom, for it not only forces them to take on international
companies and all their potential with the limited means and
strength of a national state, but also, thanks to the electoral
system, to work with guaranteed instability and insecurity.
However convinced a government politician might be that
technological progress should be less rapid, he must on the
whole ignore his conviction if he or his party are to be
re-elected.

Naturally, no business manager or politician will publicly
acknowledge that this is the case – least of all the politician,
who must appear to be independent and full of initiative –
but the indirect evidence that the conclusion is correct is so
overwhelming that even the most indignant protests are
insufficient to convince one to the contrary.

To sum up: the major problem of the advanced industrial

society is not dwindling resources, an overworked environment or the other adverse manifestations of highly commercialised civilisation. These are merely symptoms. *The fundamental problem of our civilisation is that its political and economic structure is out of date.* The explanation for unchecked development is not to be found in dynamic qualities such as man's urge to progress, his curiosity or his desire for material things. Rather must it be sought in the structure and functioning of the image of reality we have formed; in the first place, therefore, in the political and economic system which we must admittedly maintain in some form if a developed society is to function at all, but which in its present condition is unsuited to the demands which modern technology makes upon it. It is probably true to say that the image has taken command of mankind, and equally accurate to assert, with Marx, that technology has a tendency to grow away from the conditions of production under which it is developed. Technology therefore takes over, and we consequently lose our ability to control it.

In the present situation it seems that we can distinguish only between those parts of the social system which are governed and those which govern. This is not to say that some people make decisions without being keenly aware of limitations on their freedom to act, while others merely do as they are ordered. Even the most powerful politicians and businessmen in the major countries have to act within a framework so narrow that, even now, it would belie talk of real freedom of action.

This does not imply that, for instance, technical developments at company level have taken over. Every day conscious decisions are made by boards of directors, managers and production experts. However, the responsibility for the new technology and its consequences cannot be assigned to specific persons or organisations, no matter how powerful they may be or to what extent they may dominate the market. If the company he is appointed to direct is to survive, the director of a firm in a market economy cannot choose a line of development different from that which he believes to be the most profitable in the long run. It is not, primarily, a question of the background or social status of the decision-maker. All things considered, we shall not have a different pattern of development, a less uninhibited exploitation of natural resources or a more humane technology, merely by admitting employees to the board of directors or by any other method of democratising the decision-making process. The dominant power of the owners is undoubtedly unjust and must be broken, but it would be naïve to believe that by so doing we would have created the basis for a more humane technology or a slower rate of growth. At the present level of development, decisions as to what will be produced and at what level the growth rate is to be maintained, are governed by the capitalist system's structure and manner of functioning, both of which are essentially independent of the people directing this system and working within it. If we are of the general opinion that technological developments are taking a direction or having consequences we find unacceptable, it is tantamount to saying that the political and economic organisations are imperfect and must be changed.

Far-sighted politicians are gradually improving social conditions, but rapidly diminishing resources, the threat to the environment and all the other disadvantages of the industrialised society make it imperative to change the present course of events. This is a task which can no longer be carried out within the framework of a virtually unaltered political and economic organisation. Our ship will be stranded on the rocks because we have never been able to gain control of the rudder.

If we had a price system which, in the true sense of the word, could equitably control the use and exploitation of resources, then capitalism would be the superior system; we would have precisely the growth and type of production for which there was scope and demand. But it does not work like this, and it would be a dangerous and unacceptable strategy to follow the liberal pattern and patch up and manipulate the price system, and then assert that all will be well.

If the growth and content of production conflict with the situation created by scarce resources, a sensitive environment and, for that matter, public demand, other means must be employed.

(1) The most important point in all the demands is that uncontrolled, reckless development must be stopped. It is the political and economic organisation – particularly the far-reaching fragmentation of competing units, from international blocs to individual nations and companies – which is mainly responsible for the insatiable urge for growth.

The only possible solution to this problem demands that national objectives and egoistical motives should be replaced by an overall plan of action employing vast resources. If in future each individual nation, like the companies in a market economy, is to be allowed not only to decide freely what to do with its net profit (i.e. goods and services not needed to maintain present assets) but also to make a constant effort to increase it, this of itself will produce a technological development pattern of the same type as has been known hitherto, with all the concomitant implications of increasing exhaustion of resources, environmental damage, unemployment and discrepancies of income between developed and developing countries.

This is a plea for a completely different global structure. It will only be completed after a very long period – perhaps not for several hundred years – but it is clear that it will be carried out stage by stage, for, at our present level of technology, this is our only hope of controlling developments. In practice, the political independence of the smaller national states will be the first thing to be questioned and restricted.

Along with the transformation of global political organisation, the capitalist economic system's entire structure and manner of functioning must be changed. Far-reaching alterations must be made to the system of a market economy.

(2) The unheeding independence of capitalism must be restricted. Even at a national level the community must be able to insist on the type of production desired, but, even more important, it must be able to ensure that progress is made at the pace required in any given situation. The ability to guide in this way depends on the community taking control of the dynamic elements in the market economy – the forces pushing production upwards and the influence of competition. Progress must not be stopped, but it must be guided much more rigidly than at present, and probably by other means than those tried so far.

Applied research and development activities and, in the final analysis, the search for fresh knowledge, are more difficult to control and stop, either temporarily or partially. Pseudo-development and market manipulation can be limited, and competition can be halted. One or two levels in the progression from basic research to adaptation to the market or the market itself can quite consciously be monopolised. The Swedish railway monopoly has made possible a relatively slow-paced and, most important, controlled technological development. By means of a combination of subsidies, reconstruction and functional downgrading, the rolling stock has been utilised throughout the whole of its technical life-span. Without doubt, a Western European railway monopoly would provide far-reaching opportunities for guiding developments and ensuring that these took place at a suitable rate. This would be even more effective in the hypothetical case of there being a global railway system.

The significance of competition as a driving force has been underestimated, partly because we are misled by the trend towards monopolisation at a national level. The truth is that even the biggest multinational company is exposed to fierce competition which forces it to adopt ever more efficient technologies and increasingly sophisticated market-ing techniques. While this has certainly led to a higher material standard with more and better products, other consequences have been wasted resources, damage to the environment and the constant increase of other negative repercussions. The effects of competition must in future be examined more carefully and it is likely that freedom for increasing and rationalising production and developing new products within the framework of what is possible will have to be severely limited in some way or other. In practice, planned production and growth in the true sense of these terms will only be feasible and fully implemented when we have reached the point where control of companies in any specific branch can be carried out in a co-ordinated fashion and, irrespective of nationality, within the framework of one and the same system of economic and political rules.

(3) The acceleration of growth will be stopped whether we want it or not, thus halting the exponential growth in the production of goods and services and consequently requiring the economy to be brought into balance. It is possible that the capitalist economic system, which in its purest form must expand, will be so undermined by the necessity of gradually adapting to a state of balance as to create a situation where what remains could scarcely be called a mixed economy. What we do know for certain is that the present-day situation strengthens the already growing demand for society's intervention in the allocation of resources.

(4) The distribution of resources must be qualitatively efficient. This is not merely an efficiency associated with such concepts as productivity, stress or specialisation, but rather with ideas such as the supremacy of necessity, recycling, selectivity, saving, and reducing over-production. The need for quality will find its concrete expression in the influence directly or indirectly exerted by society upon the ultimate decision concerning what is to be produced.

The most effective instrument in the hands of the community for forcing production into more meaningful areas is the right use of public pressure within the framework of rules created by a market-dominated economy. Theoretically, the government can also ensure that where, for some reason or another, certain sectors or projects are considered inappropriate, the supply of external resources is curtailed or stopped completely. The likelihood of making a profit on undesirable production can be limited, and there are well-known technocratic methods of governing production.

There is also another longer-term possibility, perhaps only theoretical, on which we have already touched. The feasibility or otherwise of ensuring that the technological bases were removed, or at least were not used, is a provocative thought, pointing to a philosophical problem in that it touches on the unrestricted right to seek knowledge. In the new position in which humanity finds itself, however, there are fields of knowledge which – as has been argued – it is best not to exploit at all, or, at the very least, to exploit with great caution. The power of the possible is worth watching.

A further point must be added. Time is short, and it may well be that most of the tasks listed will have to be such that very soon much of what we now consider right and proper, important and relevant, or even merely suitable at the present moment, might be seen to be wrong, unfitting, marginal or unsuited to the current situation. National neutrality and the right of self-determination have been highly honoured concepts, but soon they might be seen in the reverse context as expressions of reaction and limited vision. It might be that monopoly is something to be aimed for, and that multinational companies will be an asset. The search for knowledge for its own sake might be a virtue today but a vice tomorrow.

Another down-to-earth way of deciding how far we are from conventional thinking is to ask whether the economic and political questions current in the highly industrialised and capitalist part of the world today are relevant to the problem indicated here. How important is legislation aimed at ensuring a minimum wage or a fair distribution of incomes when two-thirds of the world's population is hungry, and when the labour market for the most highly-paid section of the population is internationalised, thus making a policy of fair distribution of incomes ridiculous? Can this absurd disproportion not be explained merely on the basis of the short-sighted political system we now enjoy?

How relevant is opposition to worker representation on the boards of directors, in a situation in which the pre-rogative of ownership as such is not even a historical prece-dent, and in any case is based on uncertain grounds; in which the individual firm's freedom of action is severely restricted, and the seriousness of the present position demands that all should work together? A spokesman for business or industry who, in principle, rejects the idea of worker representation by pointing out that if such a course of action is followed, then the present system of owner or director responsibility will no longer function, is displaying a very limited understanding of a new situation. "The whole of our legal apparatus is based on this system, and no one is likely to take the first step to change the legal system." Does Axel Iveroth really believe that the legal system is a divine institution?

How much weight can be attached to the question of the work environment when we know that not only individual firms and branches of industry, but the whole of business and industry in a country must work in accordance with the conditions prevailing in the developed industrial society, conditions which can be only marginally affected by a single nation? Can the influence ever be anything but marginal so long as people are subordinated to technology and its demands for conformity and adaptation?

Can politicians' opposition to the accession of a single country to a larger economic community be said to be particularly in line with developments? Are they not confus-ing the aims and methods of the present moment with those of the future? How probable is it that the larger community will be any more adept at avoiding a global programme of action than the country which lies outside the boundaries of the community? How much honesty and how much political weakness can be discerned when accession is allowed in practice but not officially? In his play, *Saint Joan*, Bernard Shaw includes a scene in which an English chaplain and an English nobleman are discussing a French nobleman's military prowess:

> *The Chaplain.* He is only a Frenchman, my lord.
> *The Nobleman.* A Frenchman! Where did you pick up that expression? Are these Burgundians and Bretons and Picards and Gascons beginning to call themselves Frenchmen, just as our fellows are beginning to call themselves Englishmen? They actually talk of France and England as their countries. Theirs, if you please! What is to become of me and you if that way of thinking comes into fashion?
> *The Chaplain.* Why, my lord? Can it hurt us?
> *The Nobleman.* Men cannot serve two masters. If this cant of serving their country once takes hold of them, goodbye to the authority of their feudal lords, and goodbye to the authority of the Church.

It looks as though the questions to which, in the shelter of the nation, we devote a great deal of attention, and to which we ascribe considerable importance, are in fact quite secondary and unreal in the broader perspective: it would also seem that the answers we give are often reactionary and intolerable. Perhaps the following questions could be considered as important for the future:

(1) In an independent nation how is it possible to persuade people to accept that the country's freedom of action in all essential matters should be subjected to the decisions of supra-national institutions within a few decades?

(2) What measures should be introduced in the global economic system to ensure that developments are quantitatively controlled?

(3) How can measures be taken in the global economic

system to ensure that the production of goods and services is also qualitatively well balanced?

(4) By what methods can we adapt ourselves to an economy which is in a state of stagnation?

(5) How can we best achieve a balance between, on the one hand, the irresistible and increasing present-day pressures towards increased centralisation, central planning and inflexibility and, on the other, the fundamental demand for decentralisation and flexibility?

Any one of these tasks would demand such a high degree of solidarity, vision and renunciation that to realise them all would signify a unique achievement on the part of the established forces. Never before in history has power voluntarily been surrendered to others; what has previously appeared to be a voluntary relinquishment of power has, in fact, been only almsgiving. Alms are no longer sufficient and, in any case, time has finally run out.

The society we should try to fashion

Now to consider what must be done. From here we can begin to discern the outline of a different form of society which we must gradually build up – a "vision".

When in 1967, at the age of 90, Arnold Toynbee was confronted with Haight-Ashbury in San Francisco – the first emergence of the hippie culture – his words caught the attention of the shocked and disturbed establishment. He argued that it is best to listen and learn, for he felt that the new culture was, fundamentally, an important phenomenon indicating that our highly developed society had gone too far. He maintained that the hippie movement should not be seen as an alternative way of life but as a symptom that to some people our own way of life has become "sick" and unacceptable.

There was such an outburst of protest at this that it is difficult to discern a distinct pattern of fundamental unity in the attacks. However, disregarding such things as objectives, the current situation, the location and party-political overtones, there is still a common denominator which can be summed up as the unreserved criticism of the entire establishment by the youth of the world. No political ideology is spared. As Roger Garaudy has very honestly pointed out, eruptions of student protest are not solely a phenomenon of capitalist countries. The national political administration is distrusted and criticised at both central and local levels. Central organisations, both professional and co-operative, are accused of bureaucracy and betrayal, and of displaying patriarchal attitudes towards their members and their fundamental ideas. The industrial and military establishments are commonly supposed to have values and to carry out actions which are rejected and condemned. It would appear that no established group, anywhere, escapes the attack and its accompanying good measure of contempt. Common expressions thrown in their direction are "chauvinism", "centralism", "bureaucracy", "lack of freedom", "remoteness", "inhumanity", "cynicism" and "brutality".

Such criticism is justified and should be endorsed. There seems to be a movement towards a polarisation of the community, in which a decreasing number of people govern the rest. The relative balance and conflict between different established groupings, which has persisted for at least a century, has been replaced by co-operation and understanding between them.

The political, economic and cultural influence of the minority has probably never been greater than it is today. Even though, in relative terms, there has been a more equitable distribution of incomes from the established economic forces (whether they are called feudalism, mercantilism or industrial capitalism) over the centuries, it has been, more than anything else, a redistribution among the socially better-off classes. This is probably true, on the whole, of other forms of influence. Perhaps it is a gigantic myth that we have in the main been freed from the yoke of economic, political and cultural ties to the actions and standards of an élite minority – such as historically has been the case so far. Suppose it were possible to point to the thousand people most influential today and a hundred years ago, it might well transpire that the establishment of today was able to carry out its intentions much more rapidly and determinedly than that of 1872. The fact that an expanding economy has given us a materially better life need not necessarily conflict with that assumption. The fact that irrespective of sex, race or financial position we have the right to vote is no indication that the assumption is incorrect. Equally, the fact that people living in most countries have both mental and physical freedom of action should not prevent us from appreciating that the power of the oligarchy today is more complete than ever before.

This conclusion is supported by the indisputably closer relationship developing between the state and the business world which is characteristic of all advanced capitalist societies. (In this respect a socialised economy is naturally already "highly developed".) Seen in a historical perspective this process is not unique. At least in the capitalist era the interrelationship amongst economic, spiritual and political authorities has generally been adapted to the conditions and desires of the economic forces.

Jan Myrdal asserts that India's cows were declared sacred not because of some early religious prescript, but for simple economic reasons. Religion has gradually adapted to this and made its contribution. Historians appear to be agreed that capitalism simply bought the understanding and connivance of the Church, and indeed in the fourteenth and fifteenth centuries it was common for wealthy bankers to finance the work of the Church. Nor is that all – the Reformation produced new and highly adapted ethical rules, this being the contribution of Calvinism rather than Lutheranism. The Protestant doctrine of hard work and simplicity led indirectly to the accumulation of capital. Hard work meant a good income, simplicity meant low consumption and savings, and savings led to a growth of wealth which was then applied to producing even greater wealth. "To become rich was never the object of a genuine Protestant, but it could well become the unexpected result."

In a similar manner the historical perspective shows an interrelationship between the economic and political forces which in many ways has been strengthened by technical and economic development. An advanced industrial economy presupposes a kind of symbiosis between the state and the business world, with constant agreed solutions, and it therefore becomes pointless to criticise the Swedish government for co-operating with private industry in such projects as the Asea Atom and Uddcomb. If we wish to have a profitable reactor industry in Sweden, then the State and private enterprises *must* co-operate. There is no other way.

It is the economic system which decides, and the politicians are really only pawns in the game. When Sven Fagerberg allows Olof Myhre to say that no decision taken in Tamania is to the disadvantage of high finance, this may be true, yet in its implied criticism of politicians it is like kicking someone who is already down. What is known as the military industrial complex (found not merely in the USA but also in socialist countries, as Roger Garaudy has equally honestly pointed out), is part of the same pattern adapted – as are training policies, labour market policies and research policies – to the demands of the highly industrialised community. For most countries the creation of capital becomes a more and more important question when individual savings in the household and in businesses are no longer sufficient to provide for the financial demands of industrial development. The State has to take a hand, and this inevitably leads to co-operation and common responsibility between state and business community. So many examples can be quoted that the picture leaves the observer in no doubt that the forces militating for an increased interdependence between economic and political/administrative groupings are extremely powerful.

Widespread disapproval of such a development would not be unreasonable. Decisions are taken without reference to people – in ministries, in the canteens of parliaments and in boardrooms. The characteristic terms used are lobbying, jollying along, political relations, nepotism, the state of the government, state subsidy and so on. It might be more important for economic progress to have good contacts in a suitable department than to make a good job of producing and marketing. Galbraith has made the valid point that it is not the ideology but the engineers which are the enemy of the market. Nor is that all. The form of society created by these means widens the distance between the leaders and the led, for it is a question of developing a still more advanced and gigantic technology.

People wish to dissociate themselves from the way of life which will inevitably follow: a fragmented, dehumanised, constantly changing and planned society with little scope for what most of us consider to be important – a total perspective, personal contacts and sympathies, private initiative, stability and flexibility. It is wrong almost to the point of cynicism to talk of anti-intellectualism in the protest movement. At most it can be said to be a dissociation from the special form of intellectual activity which is related to research and development in the Western world, but the most elementary anthropological knowledge shows that the sacrosanct character of industrial activity is not so obvious in all civilisations.

The growing criticism from outside is aimed at all phenomena which can be associated with an extension and strengthening of the existing industrial form of society. It is immaterial whether it is a question of socialist or capitalist economies: as has been remarked, nationalisation and corporativism are by and large different terms for the same thing, and it is their repercussions in which people are interested. This is almost certainly what François Mauriac was getting at.

Some people might be shocked to discover that none of the

qualitative features needed are to be found in continued industrialisation *according to the present pattern.* By means of a great effort we might raise material production slightly for a few decades without worsening the working environment, without causing increased urbanisation, gigantomania, alienation or stress, but this would be doing things unnecessarily badly during the short period of respite which is all we can count on.

The society we are seeking is the land of Erewhon. There is no way back to a life of increasing material standards, virtually unlimited mental and physical freedom, small organisations and no interrelationships. This is and will remain a Utopian dream. Nevertheless, there are presumably intermediate forms at which we can aim, qualitatively far superior to the advanced industrial society. An elementary analogy might give an idea of how these could be attained.

All technology, all technological methods, all knowledge can, with a degree of simplification and a little imagination, be said to be an extension and refinement of the resources mankind was given by Nature. With the help of spectacles we are able to see better. With the help of roads we are able to move about more quickly. With the help of pens, books and libraries, we are able to "remember" better. This could be called the implemental dimension of technology. However, implements and tools can be used in different ways; we can organise our work, at least, according to two main patterns. It appears that the principal decision on this was made when some nations – those which have subsequently become materially successful – decided at some stage to base their production on a division of work and profit. In this sense the organisation of labour is the second dimension in technology, which like the first can be said to be universally true because it has applied to people ever since they began to use tools to help them in their work. A third dimension has recently been introduced – the right of ownership of technology. Through this the community, individuals or companies all have the right to determine the use of technology and its products.

It looks as though developments have now progressed so far that the implemental dimension is more important than the other two. The technology which characterises the developed industrial society can only be used and fashioned according to a pattern and, even more important, is outside the influence of those who formally own it. Technology looks the same in both capitalist and so-called socialist states. If we wish to change the conditions of life in a developed society, we are forced to bring technology to heel. Technology determines how society is to look. Our vision must be focussed on the chance to fashion a different kind of technology.

We must bring technology to heel

In his work, man has gradually been subordinated to technology. The craftsman has become a machine tool operator, and this transformation represents a step from a certain degree of independence and responsibility to programming and conformity. The individual has been forced to assume increased responsibility for a fragment of his production – an expensive piece of machinery or a complex partial operation – but, at the same time, he is finding it more and more difficult to point to, let alone demand, responsibility from whoever is in charge of the firm as a whole. Technology is dehumanising the management of men, and presents an overall picture of the privilege in the hands of a small and elusive minority. Technology much prefers to see a conscientious, careful and attentive worker in the right place, ready to press the right button at the right time. If people are not prepared to accept this kind of role, they are replaced by a more independent kind of technology. Rightly or wrongly, this trend leads to insecurity. In addition one has to reckon with the fact that noise, cold, heat and accidents are still factors to be taken into account in many places of work.

The individual situation in the place of work is repeated on a larger scale in the community as a whole. The landscape is refashioned according to the demands made by, for instance, modern communications technology in the form of cars, underground railways and aeroplanes. Almost without exception, motorways, tunnel exits or airports are built where the technocrats want them to be built, and according to the pattern already followed in New York City, Tokyo or Moscow. It is difficult, if not impossible, to judge whether or not the proposals are reasonable, since no politician – let alone a layman – has either the time or the knowledge to force his way through the technocrat's armament of jargon, statistics and formulae. The real responsibility disappears into an impenetrable and diffuse corps of civil servants. Who knows the head of the department or the planning engineer who started the process? In his turn, however, the technocrat himself is only the tool of technology. It is the modern community's demand for good communications which forces these and similar changes upon us, and the civil servants have merely to carry out the tasks with which developments confront them. In this situation no one can take much notice of the opinions expressed by people in general.

Violence, increasingly powerful and strident protests against these developments on the part of extra-parliamentary groups, and distrust of the representatives of the establishment are symptoms of a sick society. It is technology which the illness has attacked and deformed, and it will not be healed until the imperfect economic and political system – which is the initial cause of the illness – is changed so that the further development and use of technology can be influenced.

Since people are not prepared to accept its repercussions, the fact that technology must be changed becomes particularly obvious when we talk of the right to work. If we continue to exploit and especially to fashion technology as

we have done so far, no society will be in a position to offer
its citizens full employment. This has already been demonstrated. According to Jan Myrdal, unemployment is spreading all over the capitalist world. Now is the time to ask
where talk of planned social development is taking us. What
became of the promises of an economy without crises?
Myrdal could have said that, today, workers are being
dismissed everywhere, irrespective of whether they are in
capitalist or socialist economies. Now is the time to ask . . .

The employment situation in the non-industrialised
countries is even more significant – technology's effects on
employment and in the community as a whole are even more
noticeable here. Despite the often impressive progress towards industrialisation made by many developing countries,
unemployment and under-employment have not even been
reduced, let alone eradicated. With the help of modern
capital-intensive technology, in which the investment per
job is normally something like £10,000 (not taking into
account the necessary associated investments on the part of
the community), the capital which the Indian economy can
produce is simply not sufficient to provide work for more
than a fraction of all those wanting it. In point of fact, a
policy aimed at solving the employment crisis by methods
based on Western technology (which is also being done by
the so-called socialist countries) is unreasonable and unrealistic. It is equally obvious that if the technology required
costs only an average of £5,000 or £1,000 per job, then
twice as many or ten times as many jobs would be made
available for the same amount of capital.

Since, in the short term, capital is the most serious
limiting factor for a developing country, the choice of
technology will decisively affect the number of people given
work – this is the simple basis for the argument that if we
wish to give employment to as many people as possible we
should strive to change our technology. This will be the
more suitable course to follow, since the speed with which
the world's natural resources are being exhausted at the

moment precludes the possibility of industrialising the developing nations to the extent, and with the technology, known in the developed countries. Not even the most massive aid programme on the part of the industrialised countries, based on highly developed technology, would be able to remove the problem of unemployment and under-employment; indeed, it would never be possible to carry out such a programme.

Should not the discussion concerning the kind of help to be given to underdeveloped countries today be centred more on the choice of technology than is at present the case? Irrespective of the questions of employment and resources, is it really justifiable for the developed countries to seek to hand on a form of civilisation which is being questioned more and more by those who have experience of it? Is not the lack of a work force, which has been brought up on the specific demand for conformism and rationality made by technology today, really an asset rather than a weakness for a country? In any case, there should be plenty of reasons why developing countries should not accept all the developed countries' technology and industrial bases without question. Are the products resulting from modern technology, and originally developed in and adapted to a form of society with radically different foundations, particularly useful to a developing country? Is a crash programme, aimed at creating cells of highly effective production units which are only loosely linked to the community as a whole, really anything to boast about? Who is being helped?

The less fortunate aspects of modern society and, perhaps, the demands for more meaningful employment in an acceptable environment, provide sufficient reason for taking a further look at the path followed by technology, the way in which it is being used and particularly the social conditions which allow this to happen. The decisive point, however, is that highly developed technology inevitably results in a centralised organisation of the community such as was first seen in the industrial society in England after 1830, and has since spread all over the world without regard to whether the economic sysem calls itself "mixed" or "socialist".

The growth of central administration, the shift of power from parliament to government, the tendency towards centralisation in all major organisations and in virtually every area of a capitalist country is matched in the socialist countries, and forms the basis for the universally expressed disapproval of and contempt for the entire establishment. It is important to understand the major role played by technology in bringing about this development.

Marx believed that it should be possible to create the "Socialist Man" in three stages. First, the means of production should be transferred to public ownership. After that the state should be built into a powerful unit and then, when a certain stage of material and intellectual well-being had been reached, the state should gradually wither away to mark the third stage. Many doubted whether this last stage would ever be achieved. In the ideological argument which arose between the communist Marx and the anarchist Bakunin, and which mainly concerned the relative realism of Marx's idea regarding the ultimate decline of the state, reality has shown Bakunin to be right on almost every count. Marx and, subsequently, Lenin show an almost incomprehensible naïveté in believing that – with the help of a relatively undeveloped central administration which was in any case ultimately doomed to wither away – it would be possible to cope with the problems which their programme would lay on the shoulders of the state.

Conscious attempts have been made to halt the growth and influence of the central apparatus, but in practice the forces seeking to decentralise decision-making and responsibility appear to have been weaker than the demands for concentration and central planning made by the highly developed industrialised society. In Yugoslavia, where the best-known and most far-reaching experiments have been carried out, the phase of independence and decentralisation is being concluded and succeeded by a new "integration

phase". What is implied is that aiming to combine an
economy based on a highly developed technology with
far-reaching fragmentation of the country's production apparatus into relatively small, independent units, is difficult
or impossible to carry out.

Reality has proved Bakunin to be right for the same reason
as has made it difficult for Yugoslavia and other socialist
economies to create a more decentralised and humane
society. It is not the established groups' desire for greater
power, or their reluctance to relinquish their position of
privilege, which ultimately explains the tendency to consolidation and the extension of the central governing apparatus.
The explanation is to be found in the universal manner of
using and directing technology; it is technology's particular
demand for far-reaching co-ordination, suitable training and
research and vast, concentrated efforts towards expansion
in the fields of communication and energy supplies. Even
more important is technology's need for huge resources, and
for some means of dealing with its after-effects in terms of
caring for sick and worn-out people, quickly transferring
workers from unproductive sectors and regions to firms and
parts of the country which are thought to have a bright
future ahead, and reducing environmental pollution and
wastage. Total costs for the state alone in a country like
Sweden account for 10–20 per cent of state expenditure, and
the same pattern is found in every highly industrialised
country. Moreover social services and the health service,
employment policy and protection of the environment are
absorbing a rapidly increasing proportion of the total
resources.

Ironically enough, the forces of production have grown
too powerful not only for the capitalist production situation,
but also for the kind of economic and political system which
Marx considered should be able to control them. An important reason for the fundamental failure of practical socialism
on this decisive point is to be found in the fact that, under
the pressure of the tremendous day-to-day planning problems

and the need to effectivise production as quickly as possible, there was neither time nor resources for the really essential issue – questioning whether the Western technology which they were using and developing really contributed to the creation of "Socialist Man" which was the ultimate aim.

The really crucial challenge for us is to contend with technology. This must be done by global agreement to carry out a programme of action aimed at solving the relatively short-term questions of imbalance, the environment and resources. We must develop a technology which does not merely cater for growing demands on energy and natural assets by the usual means, but also, in an entirely different manner, makes the demands on new resources small, perhaps even ensures that everything can be re-cycled and, in all important respects, guarantees a reduction in environmental pollution. Means must be made available to develop a technology which does not constantly produce a growing reserve of second-class workers – people who have to apply to special places of work, for special types of work, or to accept unemployment because modern technology makes too great a physical or psychological demand on them. It implies that the speed of change must be slowed down so that items without any technical faults will not be scrapped or under-used, and the products and environment which we create for ourselves will not be changed so quickly that we feel alienated from them. We must devise a technology adapted to the economic, social and cultural conditions necessary for the industrialisation of the Third World; in short, it must put an end to the overdevelopment of the industrialised countries and facilitate a faster rate of progress in the under-developed nations.

In the current unique situation, there is a great need for the development of this new type of technology, but time is short, and there is a palpable sense of alienation. The realisation of such a plan of action will entail a greater degree of centralisation, bureaucracy and restriction, and involve a more general lack of freedom than we have hitherto known, which we will find it hard to tolerate. This bitter medicine is probably the only one which will be effective, but the question is whether it will ever be prescribed. Are the national, political, economic and cultural establishments prepared voluntarily not only to forfeit most of their privileges, but also to take the initiative in bringing this about? Or are they going to fall into the historical pattern of fear, unwillingness, opposition and, in the last resort, violence, which has resulted every time it has been necessary to relinquish positions of privilege and power? Talk of law and order; attacks on so-called terrorist activities; the increasingly sophisticated security systems which surround their own spheres of influence; the augmented resources being made available for police and security activities in many countries: are these not signs that the pattern to be followed will be the same as ever? Is the reluctance of the cultural and political establishments to reduce the potency of the national state anything but an expression of the usual reaction which invariably appears when the ground is shaking beneath our feet?

If, however, reaction and narrowmindedness can be replaced by self-imposed relinquishment of power and ambition, it is possible that the global crisis will be averted, and that the kind of society which has already been indicated by the protest movement might begin to materialise.

The vision is of a society in which people are given the highest possible material standard allowed by a global equalisation of incomes, an acceptable environment in which to work and live, and – most important of all – a balanced relationship with Nature. It is a form of society which will strive to develop a technology freed from vast organisations, far-reaching co-operation or decision-making bodies and responsible authorities who are difficult to identify. Man is suited to small units. He is capable of many things, says Sven Fagerberg, and must be able to experience responsibility, care, fear and hope, together with other individuals who are so close that he can be in contact with them.

The vision is of a society which constantly strives to keep its social undertakings within such limits that everyone directly involved can be assured of an overall view and sufficient all-round experience, not only to be able to adopt an attitude towards any enterprise, but also to be *compelled* to take part in each decision and accept some of the ensuing responsibility. The objectives of any undertaking should be pursued to their furthest limits, and brought to the fullest fruition acceptable to those responsible. Those who are unable to acquiesce in the objectives of an undertaking should not be compelled to participate in carrying them out. We can only expect the emergence of a new and more humane society when – at the moment of accepting a specific task – each person is prepared not only to adopt an attitude towards and accept responsibiliy for the whole, of which his contribution is one part, but is also ready to act on his decision.

The vision is of a society which does not develop a technology whose demands on man and Nature are unrealistic or beyond reach, and which cannot bear its own costs. A system of cost review should be formulated which does not stop at the factory gate, and which does not operate on the principle that once the demands of the market are fulfilled its obligations are at an end. A litre of clean water – if returned in a polluted condition – should cost more than the price of supplying, using and partly purifying it. The price should not be the sum total of all capital costs for the sources of water supply, pipes, purifying plants and all special costs for the treatment of water, but one which democratic processes put at such a level as to ensure a natural balance. The basic rule should be that the cost is infinite until it can be convincingly demonstrated, in each individual instance, that Nature on its own can cope with the demands made on it if the water is returned in a dirty state. Methods of measurement should be devised which, to a far greater extent than at present, would identify those responsible for bearing the cost of the increasing number of socially destructive undertakings. The only resources to be used without cost should be those which could be multiplied and therefore – from the practical viewpoint – used without restriction. (For instance, a system is of doubtful validity if it turns knowledge into a private possession which can be bought and sold.)

A more humane work environment, a choice of products dictated primarily by quality, and the opportunity for the community to reduce its function as charwoman and watchdog, depend to some extent on how well we succeed in making every firm or product accept the real costs and profits ascribable to them. We should not, as now happens, decide who is a successful businessman, or what product is needed, merely on the basis of a fraction or fragment of the real demands on resources and the real profit. The attempt to find and then apply a more equitable system of measurement should be *one* tool with which we could fashion technology so that what we term "progress" really *is* progress.

This vision can be taken further. A form of society which places man and Nature before technology is something to strive for, a step in the right direction. It is not a condition of society which will invariably be achieved, nor has it been achieved anywhere so far. Ernst Wigforss asks in one of his books whether socialism can envisage a final objective. The answer is negative. "It looks as if it were leading *away* from something rather than *towards* something."

In the short run, practical socialism concerns technology; it seeks to attack on all fronts the political and economic system which allows technology to develop without restriction and to be fashioned without taking account of either man or Nature. It is vital to understand, however, that the uncontrolled industrial society cannot be tamed by anything but a global instrument with vast resources at its disposal. Thus a successful "socialist" policy not only implies a far more conscious and tolerant approach than hitherto, leading to withdrawal from national, fixed positions of power, but also involves seeking to bring this about. A socialism worthy of the name can no longer best be achieved within the confines of one nation and with the means at the disposal of one nation, only by such powerful, international implements as can be created when the national state has formally lost its significance.

Postscript

Books are very similar to people. Some of those we meet come to mean a great deal to us. Most of them pass by without being noticed or without making any lasting impression. A few irritate or infuriate us. Without trying to include them all, it might be worth mentioning a few people in the first group; those who, because of their overall view, analytical acumen, enthusiasm or simply their manner of presenting their ideas, have provided a foundation without which a book of this kind could never have been written.

A small number of writers offer a total perspective of global economic and political development. The resulting pictures will obviously be coloured to some extent by whether the writer is an economist or a sociologist, liberal or socialist, but they will still be pictures of the development of society – based on a tolerant intellectual view rather than on a dogmatic structure from which only marginal deviations are possible. Joseph A. Schumpeter, the economist, and Raymond Aron, the sociologist, belong in this category, and the sensitive way in which both writers compare the capitalist and socialist economic systems is attractive indeed. Schumpeter's *Capitalism, Socialism and Democracy* and Aron's *Eighteen Lectures on Industrial Society* are closely related accounts which, despite the fact that the ideas purveyed are several decades old, are still the best available to anyone wishing to be informed on the subjects dealt with in their books. Through his book *One Dimensional Man*,[10] and his almost classic essay *Repressive Tolerance*, Herbert Marcuse has convincingly pointed out the weaknesses of the liberal concept and its catastrophic consequences in an advanced capitalist society. Thus Marcuse has, perhaps more than anyone else, influenced both the balance of this book and the evaluations expressed in it. Other writers whose influence in this respect has been strong are (not in order of priority): Bertrand Russell, Leo Huberman, Arnold Toynbee, Barry Commoner, Barbara Ward, René Dubos (the last two through the book *Only One Earth*)[11], Noam Chomsky, Marshall McLuhan (who is a clairvoyant but much underrated), J. K. Galbraith and E. J. Mishan. From philosophical, ecological, linguistic and economic points of view, these authors indicate directly or indirectly that the society we have created by means of modern technology is, in essential respects, an anachronism and, what is more, that it is getting out of control. Using systematic analytical methods, a number of other writers say the same thing in perhaps even more convincing terms – Norbert Wiener, Stafford Beer, Aurelio Peccei and Jay Forrester. There is no denying that Forrester's *World Dynamics* (and its sequel, the Club of Rome's *The Limit of Growth*) are perhaps the most important books written so far in the 1970s. Three Swedish authors can also be added to the first category: Georg Borgström, Rolf Edberg and Hannes Alfvén.

Sporadic reading of Karl Marx and his contemporary, John Stuart Mill, make it plain that both these writers possessed an impressive amount of wisdom and analytical acumen. Most noticeable is the fact that the socialist Marx and the liberal Mill were so close to each other in many respects as to be almost in agreement. Arnold Ljungdal has made a better job of interpreting Marx's view of the world than anyone else I know.

Modern socialist writers such as André Gorz, Roger Garaudy and even Ernst Wigforss have had an obvious influence on the presentation. Herbert Marcuse has already been mentioned and Theodor Adorno must also be included in this category.

From differing viewpoints and with varying degrees of intensity, a number of fiction writers have also stressed the need for man to accept his responsibility, to place reality before the image of reality, quality before quantity and the whole before the parts. These are the attitudes which have served as the basis for the analysis and the programme I have sought to present in this book.

Karl-Henrik Pettersson
Groveda, September 1972

Notes

1. Norman, B. *Mannen i backspegeln*
2. Seeberg, S. *Lungfisken: En Framtidsroman* (Stockholm, 1971)
3. Johannesson, O. *The Great Computer: A Vision*, Gollancz (London, 1968)
4. Schumpeter, J. A. *Capitalism, Socialism and Democracy*, Unwin University Books (London, 1965)
5. Watson, J. D. *Double Helix*, Weidenfeld and Nicolson (London, 1968)
6. Gerholm, T. R. *Dagens Nyheter* (21 January, 1972)
7. From *Om nödvändigheten av den socialistiska revolutionen* (Stockholm, 1971)
8. Smith, A. *The Wealth of Nations*, Penguin (London, 1970)
9. Aron, R. C. F. *Eighteen Lectures on Industrial Society*, Weidenfeld and Nicolson (London, 1967)
10. Marcuse, H. *One Dimensional Man: Studies in the ideology of advanced industrial society*, Routledge and Kegan Paul (London, 1964)
11. Ward, B. and Dubos, R. *Only One Earth: the care and maintenance of one small planet*, Penguin Books (London, 1972)

Index

DATE DUE

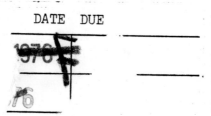